DEVELOPING
COUNSELLOR TRAINING

Developing Counselling, edited by Windy Dryden, is an innovative series of books which provides counsellors and counselling trainees with practical hints and guidelines on the problems they face in the counselling process. The books assume that readers have a working knowledge of the approach in question, and, in a clear and accessible fashion show how the counsellor can more effectively translate that knowledge into everyday practice.

Books in the series include:

Developing the Practice of Counselling
Windy Dryden and Colin Feltham

Developing Counsellor Supervision
Colin Feltham and Windy Dryden

Developing Counsellor Training
Windy Dryden and Colin Feltham

Developing Person-Centred Counselling
Dave Mearns

Developing Psychodynamic Counselling
Brendan McLaughlin

DEVELOPING
COUNSELLOR TRAINING

Windy Dryden and Colin Feltham

SAGE Publications
London • Thousand Oaks • New Delhi

SAGE Publications Ltd
6 Bonhill Street
London EC2A 4PU

SAGE Publications Inc
2455 Teller Road
Thousand Oaks, California 91320

SAGE Publications India Pvt Ltd
32, M-Block Market
Greater Kailash – I
New Delhi 110 048

British Library Cataloguing in Publication data

Dryden, Windy
  Developing Counsellor Training. –
  (Developing Counselling Series)
  I. Title II. Feltham, Colin III. Series
  361.32307

ISBN 0–8039–8942–3
ISBN 0–8039–8943–1 (pbk)

Library of Congress catalog card number 94–065540

Typeset by Mayhew Typesetting, Rhayader, Powys
Printed in Great Britain by Biddles Ltd, Guildford, Surrey

Contents

Acknowledgements

We are grateful to the British Association for Counselling for granting us permission to reproduce the (1993) edition of its Code of Ethics and Practice for Trainers; to David Smith of Regent's College, London, for permission to reproduce the Evaluation of Seminar and Tutor form; and to the Center for Cognitive Therapy, Pennsylvania for allowing us to reproduce the Cognitive Therapy Scale.

Introduction

Like its companion volumes, this book is intended to offer practical guidelines for certain aspects of counselling. In this case, our subject is counsellor training and how it may be analysed, reconsidered, systematized and if necessary improved. We hope this book will therefore appeal to trainers, intending trainers, and others involved in the planning, implementation and evaluation of counsellor training programmes. It may also be of interest to trainees wishing to understand the dynamics of the training process itself.

Counselling in its modern form is perhaps only about 50 years old, and specific models of training and supervision in counselling are younger still. Thus, in the UK, counsellor training is currently in a state of early development, if not in some respects a state of mild confusion. Training in counselling, or what is called counselling, is offered on anything from a half-day workshop to a three-year full-time postgraduate programme. Courses vary from the purely theoretical to the purely experiential, and of course training in counselling reflects what is true of the counselling field in general, that there is no consensus concerning which methods are more or less reliable, rigorous or effective.

We do not want to disguise the problems facing trainers, supervisors, trainees, intending trainees and clients and it can be a salutary experience contemplating some of the obstacles before you. The intellectual and technical challenges are taxing enough but trainers must also face the more mundane realities of the economics of counselling training. Like counselling itself, training is labour-intensive. Counsellor training does not lend itself to large lectures and mass examinations, but to small scale, closely observed, experiential learning, which demands a high trainer–trainee ratio and ample time for skill development. In many ways, learning counselling resembles the apprenticeship model of learning a craft. In order to pay for this amount of personal attention, course fees have to be reasonably high, yet low enough to attract students. Such juggling can be one of the most draining of tasks for trainers and course administrators. Add to this the rapidly increasing professionalization of counselling, with the demands of individual counsellor, supervisor and trainer accreditation and course recognition, and it becomes plain that training in this field is by definition highly stressful.

It is in this context that this book is written and while we are not claiming that it is either novel or definitive, we hope it will help to bring attention to the many important issues facing counsellor trainers today. Hopefully, it will also alert all those involved in the provision and funding of counsellor training to look more sympathetically on trainers and the level of resources they require if they are to perform their task adequately.

This book is not a training manual, although we address the area of training methods within it. Those looking for creative ideas to use on their courses are advised to consult Inskipp (1986), Dainow and Bailey (1988), Egan (1990) and Jacobs (1991). The book is also not a comprehensive A-to-Z of training issues, but it is, we trust, a fair treatment of the central considerations facing trainers who are designing or attempting to improve courses. While it is not an entrepreneur's guide to costing, setting up and profiting from training courses, we have referred to some of the literature on training from the management world, which may help to sharpen your thoughts about the counsellor training market. We have not assumed that only trainers on substantial training courses (for example, of BAC course recognition standards) will use the book, but it is largely illustrated by reference to such courses, and we hope that material relevant to shorter courses and workshops can be extrapolated. Some of the material gathered here may be well-known, but much of it is newly contextualized.

We have not gone in depth into the subject of who should be a trainer, who chooses the trainers, supervises, monitors or evaluates them, because this aspect of the field is even less well developed than the rest. We do, however, refer to some of the issues involved in gathering feedback on trainer performance, providing support and nurturance for trainers and enhancing relationships between trainers. We hope that this small volume will assist you, whether you are deciding if becoming a trainer is for you, or you are an experienced trainer seeking confirmation for many of the things you are already doing well.

We also reiterate the accepted professional custom that counselling training and re-training is an ongoing professional commitment. Some commentators have suggested that any counsellor's development into mature competency is a process taking at least 10 years and entailing many stages of learning. Russell et al. (1984) point out that while each trainee may develop at a quite different pace from their peers, this factor is neglected in counselling research and its applications to training. We look forward to seeing further research on counsellors' individual professional development and on counsellor training generally.

Windy Dryden
Colin Feltham

Improvements in the Organization of Training Courses

1 Clarify and communicate the course rationale and aims and ensure there are sufficient resources and support to carry these through

Counselling is not only fashionable but profitable for trainers and training organizations. In this climate of demand for training it is understandable that so many people seek, for excellent and sometimes not so excellent reasons, to put together and offer counsellor training courses. Given this demand, and the fact that counselling in Britain is still in an early stage of development, it is not surprising that such a wide range of courses of varying quality is to be found on offer. Courses differ considerably in length, content and quality. In this book we address mainly, but not exclusively, substantial counsellor training courses, for example spanning two or three years, part-time. If you are planning to design and run such a course, then the first questions you would be wise to consider are as follows.

1 *What are the implications of such a course being run under the auspices of my organization?*

Academic, health, religious, voluntary, commercial organizations and departments all run counsellor training courses. Many of these agencies have ideological commitments, traditions and bureaucratic structures which dictate or strongly influence the kinds of courses to be run and validated under their auspices. Counsellor training within academic departments may be required to include high levels of didactic input, intellectual content and formal examinations. Religious bodies may influence courses held under their auspices to contain a spiritual element. Courses run in health settings may wish to attract primarily health workers or provide primarily health-related counselling; or they may need to align their training with the requirements of certain health professions' examining boards. Predominantly independent, commercial courses may be required to charge high fees and to hold large classes in order to survive or prosper economically. Consider what effects such considerations will have in the short and long term on the training you wish to offer.

2   What educational, vocational, economic and other aims are involved in these plans?

Think about specific aims. Do you have in mind a training course which is heavily biased towards intellectual content? You may, for example, be planning a Master's degree course requiring a proficient grasp of theories of counselling psychology. Your intention may not be to train people primarily in the use of counselling skills. Alternatively, the brief of your organization or department may be to offer vocational training in specific aspects of counselling, for example in the field of HIV and AIDS. How comprehensive and generic a training do you wish to provide, as opposed to targeted, specific training? You may have been given a brief by a department head to expand opportunities for adult education relating to counselling in a specific geographical area. Perhaps your initial plan is to run short courses to sample the level of interest in counsellor training. Think through these factors and their implications well before you begin to advertise and enrol.

3   What level of training do I wish to provide?

Levels of training relating to counselling range from very short workshops to substantial training to standards of professional competency well in excess of 400 hours. Your intention may be simply to raise awareness about what counselling is (by means of short discussion groups) or to train numbers of professional counsellors. In the USA doctoral and post-doctoral training programmes in counselling, counselling psychology and psychotherapy are common, but in the UK there is still only a handful of Master's degree courses in counselling, although these are beginning to proliferate. You need to consider, within the constraints of your organization and your staff team, what level of training it is realistic for you to plan for. Short courses are not inferior, but they are of a different kind from longer, comprehensive courses. Much of your planning depends on staff and other resources. If you are essentially a one or two person operation, you may either need to begin modestly or to generate income to hire in a number of other sessional workers. Substantial counselling courses require a certain amount of specialist input, and you may not possess the necessary expertise to provide this yourself. Balance these factors when planning your courses.

4 What special resources do I and my organization offer to people applying to a course of the kind we are planning?

Resources and strengths may include the historical experience and reputation of an organization and its staff, its buildings, administrative support, technical equipment, and so on. An academic course may offer particular reassurance to trainees seeking certain qualifications, plus tuition by recognized authorities in the field, subsidized fees, research opportunities, computer access and well-stocked library facilities. A course run within a health setting may provide generous space, good canteen facilities, excellent variety of guest lecturers and ready access to placements. Other courses are attractive because they offer charismatic leaders, unique opportunities to study certain innovative approaches or an aesthetically pleasing or stimulating environment. You and your colleagues may have formed a cohesive team offering between you an exciting range of skills and expertise in particular theoretical orientations. More fortuitously, you may offer the only training in counselling for miles around.

You may offer specialist training, for example in HIV and AIDS or bereavement, from an organization with a respected reputation for HIV and AIDS or bereavement work. It is worthwhile conducting both training needs analyses within an organization and market research externally. Bond (1991) shows in his survey that those involved in HIV counselling, for example, preferred the concept of training in short blocks of days, with training for a day a week spread over three months ranking as second preference, and evening training ranking as least preferred. Analyse and capitalize on such information and promote your strengths in your literature.

5 What level of support and commitment do I and my organization offer to those who will enrol on these courses?

Counselling training is emotionally demanding for students. They commit a great deal of time and money to such training, and often great hopes and anxieties are involved. In addition, many people attach considerable importance to the outcome of their training as it will relate to their future career. Courses which are primarily set up to make money and not to nurture, respect and assist students to become professionally competent, do an obvious disservice. In the case of substantial courses lasting two or three years, it is vital that planning takes into account the question of whether the course will be financially stable, whether staff will provide continuity and administration will be effective. Teething problems and unforeseeable crises are one thing, but problems that could be avoided by careful anticipation are another. Stability and quality are two of the most significant aspects to take into account. How will you respond when trainees drop out and the financial viability of the course is threatened? How will you support students who suffer hardship, accidents or unexpected traumas? Unfortunately, counselling and counsellor training is not cut-and-dried, but requires flexibility and responsiveness. This in turn can mean great demands on tutors' time and on their own emotional resilience. Consider whether your courses can provide the necessary time and support for students and tutors.

6   What possible limitations or conflicts can be foreseen in what I and my organization can offer?

Since lengthy counselling courses require a great deal of forward planning and complex mechanisms for advertising, recruiting, training and assessment, care needs to be taken over your future ability to respond to all such aspects. It is not at all unusual for counsellor training courses to suffer from the economics of an institution, which suddenly imposes restrictions on spending or even decides to terminate particular courses. Policy decisions made 'from above' can have serious repercussions for the morale of tutors and students on counselling courses. We have known courses whose location, staff, facilities and syllabus have been changed half way through, generating considerable ill feeling among trainees. Course directors have been known to impose extra academic or skills modules on trainees midway through a course, allegedly in the interests of meeting new professional criteria, which entails extra fees. Although such changes are *sometimes* unavoidable, it is better to anticipate the possibility of their occurring and to give fair warning to trainees.

Certain factors are only too obvious and foreseeable. The building in which you work may be cramped or suffer from poor ventilation or poor soundproofing. There may be inadequate secretarial assistance (see Section 4). Incipient conflicts may exist between institutional heads and course tutors. An example here is where the Head of a college is seeking to expand courses and enhance the reputation of the college, and has in mind to employ tutors who are best qualified on paper and to promote courses which hold most market promise. If the existing tutors are mainly committed to training counsellors in an in-depth, specialized orientation, they may be less concerned with qualifications and market results than with personal qualities and individual competencies; this may well lead to conflict within the organization and to confusion for students.

Having thought through, discussed and decided on your training rationale and aims, and any constraints or problems, you may need to submit your proposals to a validation board. Then you can commit these to paper in the form of advertisements, course leaflets, policy documents, course syllabuses and complementary literature. If you are planning short workshops and particularly wish to consider issues of costing and marketing, consult Falloon (1992). Do not make false or misleading claims and do not issue material which is unhelpfully vague. (Do not, for example, claim that you offer 450 tutor-contact hours if in fact a good many of these hours are coffee breaks.) Consider the kinds of headings which will summarize what you offer, for example:

1 Course title.
2 Awards, if any, and awarding body.
3 Course venue/s.
4 Level of training.
5 Duration, dates, mode of attendance and total hours.
6 Fees.
7 Entry criteria.
8 Application procedure.
9 Staff details.
10 Aims of the course.
11 Learning/teaching methods.
12 Assessment criteria and methods.
13 Core theoretical model.
14 Skills training.
15 Course philosophy and rationale.
16 Self-development/personal therapy expectations.
17 Practical work with clients.
18 Supervision arrangements.
19 Professional and ethical issues.
20 Institutional resources and facilities.

You may add to this list or condense elements of it, or it may be that if you are offering a short course, some of these headings do not apply. We recommend that you consult BAC's booklet outlining requirements for courses which are intended to be presented for BAC Course Recognition (BAC, 1990a) and that you inspect a number of course descriptions, many of which are helpfully gathered in, for example, the *Guide to Training Courses in Counselling* (ASC, 1992). See, too, BPS (1993) and Abram (1992). Those counsellors and counsellor trainers who are preparing to launch into commercial training would do well to consider the kinds of market considerations spelled out by Thomas (1992).

Key point

Analyse your reasons for offering counsellor training, consider carefully whether you can deliver what you promise in the short and long term and then publicize accurately what your courses consist of.

---

2 Decide and implement clear entry requirements and interview procedures, in combination with clear information for candidates on the course itself

The aims and rationale of your courses dictate to some extent what your entry requirements will be. If you need to train a lot of people in a short time within an organization, then there may be no entry requirements. If your brief is to generate as much income as possible, then you are likely to have very broad entry requirements (the most important being, perhaps, an ability to pay the course fees!). In this section we mainly address trainers who have to decide on and implement some form of assessment of candidates' suitability for courses, whether these are short or long courses. In addition to what is presented here, you are advised to compare course literature from diverse sources or to read Purton's account of four such courses and their selection procedures (Purton, 1991).

Formal requirements

If it is your responsibility to recruit trainees on to a postgraduate diploma or Master's degree programme, then you are probably bound to accept applications only from candidates with specified previous qualifications and experience. If your institution has an explicit policy that only those people with a first degree can apply, then the task of excluding some candidates is made easier. When it is specified that people with first degrees or equivalent may apply, you have to decide what the 'equivalent' embraces. Where there are requirements for previous work experience, or previous basic counselling skills training, you must decide on your criteria. Will you only entertain applications from those from the so-called 'core professions' (for example, social work, nursing, teaching) or will you have a wider net, or a highly discretionary set of criteria? If you ask for previous work or life experience, what constitutes such experience? Do you have formal definitions agreed among your staff team or will you leave it to 'intuition'? Do you have a policy on English language speaking? As far as we know, there are no non-English-speaking counselling training courses in Britain, nor any multilingual courses. People whose first language is not English need to be able to speak and write English sufficiently well both to satisfy course requirements and to communicate with clients.

How will you know that candidates actually have the qualifications and experience they say they have? We may be reluctant to ask for such evidence because as counsellors we are accustomed to trusting people. In practice it may be rare that any candidate would lie about or misrepresent their qualifications and suitability, but newspapers have carried stories in recent years about individuals who have deliberately misled employing institutions about their qualifications in nursing and medicine, for example. A few cases are known, too, of people entering counsellor training with the clear intention of later abusing their position with clients. When you ask candidates for two written references, as most substantial courses now do, ensure that you receive these, that they are authentic and meaningful, and consider whether you might need to clarify any points further. Ask, as many trainers now do, for photocopies of certificates.

Discretionary requirements

You may believe that candidates for counsellor training should be mature in age. There is an argument, for example, that only people who have a certain amount of varied experience of work and relationships should be considered for training, since a great deal of counselling involves personal maturity, inner experience on which to call upon, and an ability to be able to respond empathically to a wide cross-section of clients. The subject of client–counsellor match implies that certain clients may have difficulty relating to a counsellor who is much younger or much older than themselves. Some trainers specify a lower age limit of 25, for example, arguing that no one younger is likely to have had sufficient life experience. Similarly, it is argued by some that an upper age limit is necessary. These are issues that you might think through before receiving applications and holding interviews. Whatever your decisions, they should be based on sound professional considerations rather than on any implicit ageist attitudes.

Depending on the setting of your course, its sponsoring authority, source of funding, and policies on equal opportunities, you may have clear views on encouraging applications from people with disabilities, those who are black, lesbian or gay, and so on. You might decide, for example, to take a certain number of people from so-called minority groups according to deeply held convictions. In this case, you might decide to waive or modify other entry criteria, such as formal qualifications. Do you compromise on certain criteria in order to promote other interests? Does your course focus on training content which implicitly marginalizes or even ignores certain groups of people? Newman (1991) and others argue that an uncritical 'white, Euro-centric psychology' is predominant in our training institutions. Fees for counsellor training are relatively high and automatically exclude people on very low incomes. You may want to consider whether you can offer any bursaries to encourage such applicants and to discourage white middle class exclusivity. Think, too, about how the times at which the course is held affect applications: do they suit or exclude mothers or others with family commitments, for example?

Let us consider another example of possible unexamined prejudice in some depth. Although there is no justifiable reason to discriminate on counsellor training courses against people with disabilities, and whose disabilities have no bearing on their ability to train as counsellors, can you offer the facilities that may become necessary if you wish to implement decisions to train people with disabilities? There is little point in accepting on to your course people who have mobility difficulties or sensory impairments if you cannot back this up with a training environment and resources which include ramps, lifts, large print materials, suitable audio-technology and other essential aids. Often compromises are made which effectively exclude people with certain disabilities; if your building is unsuitable for wheelchair access, for example, and your budget cannot stretch to necessary structural alterations, you may have reluctantly to accept that you cannot accommodate trainees with serious mobility difficulties. If you wish to investigate some of the ethical and practical issues involved, consult *Ramps Aren't Everything* (BAC, 1990b).

Personal requirements

The BAC (1990a) suggests that candidates for counselling training be considered in the light of the following criteria:

1 Self-awareness and stability.
2 Ability to make use of and reflect upon life experience.
3 Capacity to cope with the emotional demands of the course.
4 Ability to cope with the intellectual and academic require-ments.
5 Ability to form a helping relationship.
6 Ability to be self-critical and use both positive and negative feedback.
7 Some awareness of the nature of prejudice and oppression of minority groups.

Other organizations and institutions have criteria which closely match their own needs. Chad Varah, founder of the Samaritans, who offer telephone and personal befriending, has noted that Samaritan volunteers need to be patient, tolerant, interested, friendly, accepting, non-judgemental, 'a listener rather than a doer', and to demonstrate 'unfailing concern'. Varah has been concerned enough to dismiss some volunteers for instances of unreliability, lack of punctuality, a tendency to gossip, to seek power or to convert clients to their own religious or philosophical creeds (Varah, 1985). Such qualities and limitations may not become apparent at the application and interview stage, but you need to consider your views on them.

Depending upon the theoretical leaning of your course, it may be salient to look out especially for the qualities of openness or non-defensiveness, of warmth, expressiveness, curiosity, rationality and so on. Someone who shows an extreme commitment to active change and a busy, extroverted lifestyle, for example, *may be* considered more suitable for less introspectively-based training orientations. Someone who seems temperamentally to gravitate towards solitude and deep thought may appear more suitable for introspective or transpersonal training courses. Some of these qualities will not be apparent from completed application forms, but if you want to raise such possibilities, think carefully about the questions you ask on your application form. Ask, too, for a supporting personal statement from every candidate, which gives them the chance to consider and exhibit their idiosyncratic strengths and weaknesses. You will naturally want to know something of the candidate's background, including any instances of personal suffering and difficulty encountered. You will decide how significant these issues are for you and your course, but do not assume too much about the value of personal suffering or its absence. Consult, for example, some of the research and views put forward by Norcross (in Dryden, 1991a) on the notion of the 'wounded healer'. Beutler et al. (1986) provide a digest of important 'therapist variables' which might help you to consider the range of qualities desirable in counsellors. Aveline (1990) also provides a list of personal qualities sought in candidates for psychotherapy training, and speculates that therapist effectiveness may ultimately be more closely correlated with personality than with training. If he is right, then perhaps we need to give even more careful thought to interviewing than we have previously done.

Interviewing

Interviewing is a time-consuming activity which must be planned well in advance. Candidates should know as far as possible on what grounds they will or will not be invited for interview, whether there will be one or more interviews, and over what period. You have to decide, on the basis of the projected size of your intake and your knowledge of the likely market, how many interviews you will have to conduct and what the implications of this are. BAC (1990a) recommends that the core members of staff are involved in interviews. This is often taken to mean that two staff should interview each applicant. This acts as a safeguard against the subjective bias of a single interviewer and enables staff to confer. However, it also demands a great deal of staff time. If you need to interview 40 people, for example, allowing each of them an hour, 80 staff hours will be needed purely for the face-to-face interviewing. This is without accounting for the need for realistic breaks between interviews and time for reflection, collating and decision-making. This is a task which, if carried out rigorously, could occupy two staff members for two full weeks, in addition to demands on administrative staff's time.

In training organizations where staff are employed sessionally or part-time, interviewing is clearly highly problematic. There are two possible solutions. One is to short-list very accurately and ruthlessly; this is easier for those running established courses which receive a large volume of applications. The second is to consider a form of group interview. This method is sometimes favoured because it: economizes on staff time; allows staff to observe interviewees in action, relating to each other; allows for two or more staff to observe interviewees and to compare notes; and allows candidates to meet, ask questions and even to meet other current or past course trainees. A group interview can incorporate a session of information-giving, introductions, question-and-answer sessions, and informal and formal exercises and observations. Its disadvantages are that: many people do not shine in such competitive settings; many may be kept waiting if you need to devote some individual time to candidates; and often it is not made clear to candidates whether they are in fact being formally assessed. In our own experience, those who hold group interviews, 'orientations', 'familiarization exercises' or 'informal interviews' often fail to clarify the nature and parameters of the exercise. This seems to us an example of poor communication and dubious honesty.

Counsellor trainers are unlikely to have been trained in professional interviewing techniques and many of us may believe or argue that as counsellors our entire orientation and experience is geared towards being sensitive to others' qualities, needs, spoken and unspoken communication. Many counsellors strongly believe that they should decide on matters of selection intuitively: if you feel good about an interviewee, your decision will follow this good feeling; if you feel concerned about an interviewee, your negative decision will follow; and if you feel some subtle uncertainty, you may want to ask further questions, confer with a colleague or request a second interview. Like all interviewers, we may be inclined to rely too exclusively and subjectively on our own intuitions, gut feelings and prejudices. While it may not be practicable for already over-stretched trainers to spend time being trained in interview procedures and theories, we recommend that time is taken to think through the whole subject of interviewing.

Millar et al. (1992) outline the knowledge base that professional interviewers require and the ways in which selection interviews can be improved. The goals of the interview for both interviewers and interviewees need to be clarified. To what extent is the interview perceived by each party as a fact-gathering exercise, a sizing-up or a contest? It may seem that the goals of a selection interview are obvious, but this is not necessarily the case. An interviewee may genuinely be testing his or her own motivation in applying for the course; the interviewee may be comparing the course with others, or indeed with quite different life and career choices; he or she may be assuming that the interviewer is a warm, open and accepting 'typical counsellor' or a combative, critical examiner who has to be won over. The interviewer may wish to expose a candidate to harsh interview conditions to see how he or she responds under pressure; the interviewer may leave a lot of silence in order to test the candidate's feelings and initiatives; the interviewer may conduct the interview in a style that matches the theoretical orientation of the course. Each may have pre-existing assumptions or agendas which are brought to the interview simply to be confirmed or disconfirmed (for example, 'I'm sure this is a lousy course, but I'll just find out', or 'This candidate has put in an excellent application and I'm certain we'll take him, but I'll just see if there are any undisclosed or dark corners').

In their chapter on social perception, Millar et al. (1992) review research on person perception in interview situations. Interviewers' implicit personality theories tend to influence their judgements of candidates to a high degree and often on a 'first impressions' basis. Thus, if a candidate seems at the outset to respond poorly to psychodynamically-loaded questions, for example, the interviewer may well perceive subsequent responses as poorer than they actually are. It is recognized that mood and performance anxiety particularly may distort the way in which candidates present at interview. Stereotypes relating to gender and race may operate at both conscious and unconscious levels, lending either positive or negative bias to the interview. The need to gather and assimilate complex information in a short time can mean that interviewers simplify data understandably but unjustly.

For all these reasons, you may consider the usefulness or indeed the necessity of adopting an interview procedure which maximizes equality of opportunities (for example, excluding questions which are irrelevant to counselling, and varying the balance of gender and race among interviewers). Even so, time and resource constraints, and human error, mean that sometimes people are accepted on to courses who subsequently fail to flourish, and some candidates are denied a place who, on reflection, may well have performed competently. The presence of two or more interviewers may assist in the process of optimal selection. Hopefully, counsellors who interview candidates will possess the integrity, interpersonal skills and presence of mind to adjust during the interview to any distortions on their own or the interviewee's part, and openly allow for these to be addressed. You might, for example, disclose any reservations you feel about the interviewees and actively invite them to accept a 'second chance' at certain questions. (Some psychotherapy training institutes hold two separate interviews in order to explore both personal, emotional issues and theoretical aptitude.) Almost certainly, you will vary your manner of eliciting information from closed to open questions, from referring to the paper application to setting candidates challenging scenarios to consider.

You need to discover the candidate's unique understanding of counselling and training and to ascertain that they are not primarily seeking personal growth (if your course is intended as a training in professional competency). It is important to consider each candidate's readiness for training and for client work at this time (they may benefit from delaying training for a year or two) and also any factors of idealization or escapism in their choice of counselling as a possible career. Some applicants have overly rosy views of helping people, while others are seeking an escape from a boring job! It is of course helpful to give candidates an extended opportunity to tell you some of their significant life experiences and their conscious motivations for seeking training, and specifically for seeking training on your particular course. It should go without saying that interviewees deserve honest responses, clear information and helpful feedback. Will you honestly disclose to those anxious about making a living from counselling that it can be extremely tough-going to get a job or make a full-time living out of it? (see Feltham, 1993). Will you encourage applicants to shop around and compare what other courses are offering? Will you adopt the policy (demoralizing and infuriating for those concerned) of sending bland rejection letters, or will you attempt to offer constructive feedback? Will you offer people waiting list places? Consider these issues in advance in consultation with colleagues and check that your printed course information corresponds with the verbal information you give to candidates.

> **Key point**
>
> Know what your formal and discretionary entry requirements
> are, anticipate whether there are any criteria you may be
> willing to compromise on, communicate these clearly, and
> plan and conduct interviews in an informed and balanced
> manner.

3 Decide on and implement a clear, fair and professional means of assessment of trainees from the outset and ensure that trainees know the criteria involved

A well-structured interview, in which clear information is conveyed
in both directions, lays a foundation for future expectations of
trainees. Trainees should enter a course knowing that formal
assessment is an integral part of it, with a consequence being the
possibility of failure. Do not convey any vague or ambiguous
messages about the ease or probability of passing the course.
Consider, together with other tutors, exactly what your assessment
criteria are going to be and what the implications of each of these
will be.

What is to be assessed and what is not? Presumably, trainees'
personal therapy cannot be assessed in any way, for example.
Normally, trainees' experiences or performances in personal
development groups are not assessed (and this raises the question of
whether it is viable or ethical for assessing tutors to lead personal
development groups – see Section 20). Trainees' personal journals
are usually not assessed but there is some debate as to whether they
should be inspected or not. Professional logs, in which reflections
are made on work with clients, and the relationship between theory,
personal development and practice, are read but not necessarily

assessed. It is our view that supervision which takes place within or as an integral part of the course should be assessed, but we are aware that some course tutors believe otherwise. Since supervision is the main, if not the only setting in which trainees disclose details of their actual work with clients, we believe it is essential that assessing tutors know informally and formally about trainees' progress and about any serious concerns with levels of competency. This is examined further in Section 25. You may have a rationale for disagreeing with our position here, but what is crucial is that trainees are made aware of the boundaries of assessment.

Who should assess trainees' coursework? Most counsellor training involves at least a degree of ongoing assessment, often by self and peers as well as by tutors. This may be in addition to formal examinations, assignments and vivas, or it may be instead of these methods. Counselling and educational ideologies which stress student-centred values may seek to avoid any form of assessment which smacks of authoritarianism or hierarchical power. If you and your co-tutors prefer a model of trainee self-assessment and/or peer-assessment, consider how formal or informal this will be, and how binding trainees' decisions will be. If individual trainees and their peers rate themselves as competent, while you have serious misgivings, will you still accept 'majority rule' or will you exercise a right to veto? We advocate a mixture of ongoing, trainee self- and peer-assessment and ongoing and periodic tutor-made assessments. Obviously assessments carried out by tutors, in a field like counselling which rests on many subjective variables, risk being biased. Such bias can be, and in our view should be, balanced by marking being done by more than one tutor, and representative samples of all formally assessed work being checked by an external examiner. Even so, you will need to decide on whether certain assignments carry more weight than others or whether you will initiate an averaging-out system of assessment.

How much flexibility in assessment will you allow? You need to consider what you will do in the event that trainees who are excellent interpersonally fail written assignments, or vice versa. Will you instigate a system of vivas (face-to-face interviews allowing trainees to explain and explore their strengths and weaknesses)? Will you allow second chances, giving some trainees the opportunity to re-submit pieces of work? Another difficult issue, connected with institutional pressures, concerns decisions and compromises where certain trainees may have been funded to come on the course by institutions with which you have politically sensitive links. Will you make it plain that tutors' professional judgement in assessing trainees' suitability to be declared competent counsellors cannot be compromised under any circumstances?

What systems of measurement will you use? We advocate some formal assessment of the skills and theoretical parts of counselling training. The assessment of skills development has many implications for the size of groups of trainees and for the criteria to be used (see Section 14). The BAC suggests that a minimum requirement of 10,000 words of formal written material is made on substantial courses (BAC, 1990a). Written assignments obviously have to be read and assessed according to understood criteria. It is useful to acquaint trainees with these criteria at the outset, and they might include:

1 A demonstrated understanding of the significance of the particular subject.
2 An ability to grasp and conceptualize the core ideas and/or texts involved in an assignment.
3 An ability to structure thoughts and arguments, using appropriate introductions, subheadings, conclusions, references, etc.
4 A demonstrated understanding of the personal significance of material, using examples from their own or their clients' lives (that is, from the 'real world').
5 An awareness of how particular subjects relate to others, especially to other course components.
6 A critical awareness of the scope and limitations of particular models, approaches and authors.
7 An acceptable level of accuracy in conceptualizing and referring to significant texts.
8 An ability to internalize substantially and to 'own' the relevant concepts and their implications.

Where more than one tutor is marking assignments, guidelines like these can be referred to. In combination with this, you must decide on a marking system. Many counsellor trainers dislike numerical gradings, partly on the grounds that they are too subjective and partly because they do not reflect and honour the student-centred ethos of counselling. Marking is not even entertained at all by some strictly student-centred courses. If you decide that you will utilize marking, or you are obliged to because of the nature of your institution, be clear about its meaning and parameters. Some tutors advocate a simple pass or fail system. Pass, fail and distinction is another common system. Where numerical systems are used, it makes little difference what the scale is, so long as it is understood where the pass, fail or distinction levels are. You may use a range of 1 to 5, 1 to 10 or percentages. If you use this kind of system, decide clearly what constitutes a fail (40 per cent, 45 per cent, 50 per cent?) and a distinction (65 per cent, 70 per cent, 75 per cent?). Decide at least roughly, in collaboration with other tutors, how to rate assignments in the middle band. For example, 45 per cent may represent a minimally acceptable level of the criteria outlined above (that is, points 1 to 8); 50 per cent may represent satisfactory; 65 per cent may represent a well above-average level; 70 per cent may represent a distinction. Another system is: satisfactory, good, very good, or similar, broadly indicative bands. Ensure that your guidelines are conveyed to the external examiner, who should be sent a representative sample (for example, 25 per cent) of the best, worst and average assignments.

You must decide on whether any piece of work carries extra weighting, or even the possibility of a complete pass or fail attached to it. Take the case of a male student who passes all other assignments, individually or on average, but who fails to satisfy your criteria in his submitted tape-recording and/or transcript of a session. Do you fail him altogether, allow him to submit a second tape, to attend a viva or submit further mitigating evidence of his competency? Will you decline to award a Diploma but grant a Certificate of Attendance? If one of your trainees demonstrates high levels of interpersonal skill but performs badly on written assignments, will you devise a weighting system which none the less allows him or her to pass the course and receive an award? Think through the implications of each of these courses of action. You may want to be fair to current trainees, but you need to protect the reputation of the course for holding real standards. You may want to acknowledge certain students' exceptional needs, but in doing so you may risk charges of favouritism and pliable standards. Ask yourself what meaning you, and the professional community, attach to the certificates and diplomas you offer.

It is also necessary to decide on minimal attendance requirements and to establish policies for unforeseeable illness, personal crises, pregnancy and so on. Will you agree to trainees taking time out, to be balanced by extra assignments or examination re-sits, or instead offer the opportunity of rejoining the course the following year? Anticipate too the eventuality of trainees failing who contest your decision and request an appeal. What system of appeal will you establish? Ensure that you have a well thought-through procedure for your examining board to decide on such policies in general and on individual cases in particular. Use the resources offered by your external examiner. Unfortunately it is not possible to anticipate every possible anomaly, but cover as many of these scenarios as you can in your planning and publicize them fairly and unambiguously to your trainees. Consider too the practice, used on some courses, of consulting students on all these issues. Discover by discussion and questionnaire, for example, what students believe to be fair and effective assessment criteria. See Appendix 2 for a specimen of assessment criteria.

Key point

Consider the many aspects of assessment that you will need to contend with, establish clear policies and any areas where discretion is valid, and make this information available to trainees as early in the course as possible.

---

4 Ensure that the physical learning environment and administrative systems and personnel enhance rather than impede training

Training courses can stand or fall on the environment in which they take place. No amount of excellent training from skilled trainers can make up for a training environment being cold, noisy, unwelcoming and uncomfortable. You may be tempted to try and 'make do' with poor premises, but sooner or later this will become an obstacle. Consider the quality of access to your training venue. Is it so far away from public transport that only car drivers can attend? If so, is there anywhere to park? If the course takes place in the evening, is lighting good and is the area safe? Women, in particular, may not feel safe if the training venue is in an isolated, poorly lit location, which is poorly served by public transport. We have already mentioned the question of access for those with disabilities (see p. 10). How user-friendly is the building you propose to use for your training? These questions imply marketing considerations (no one will buy your product if it is unattractive) but also psychological and ergonomic issues. An unwelcoming building will not foster a warm, trusting, learning climate. Hard chairs and thin walls do not make for concentration and accurate listening. Your trainees will not feel adequately respected if it seems they are being fobbed off with substandard accommodation, and such feelings are important when you are trying to instil the significance of respect into future counsellors.

Compromises often have to be made between ideal and attainable goals in the matter of training accommodation. Ideally you would have a purpose-designed suite of rooms. They would be tastefully designed, incorporating good heating, lighting and ventilation systems. They would include large whole-group training rooms, a number of smaller seminar rooms and one or two small consulting rooms. All rooms would have sufficient soundproofing, comfortable carpeting, optimally supportive chairs and floor cushions. You would have state-of-the-art moving whiteboards, audio and video equipment, photocopying, library and computer facilities. Trainees would have easy access to refreshment-making facilities and other convivial supports, such as a canteen, telephones, toilets, etc. Is this what your training environment looks like? Probably not. It is not unusual to have to compromise, making do with rooms that are not quite large enough for the number of trainees, chairs which are too hard or soft, lack of double-glazing, unpredictable access to equipment, and so on. The more of the former conditions you can provide, the better. The more you have to compromise, and the more you accept such compromises, the worse this bodes for the reputation of your course among current and future students. If your premises are seriously lacking in certain facilities, then you must plan to improve them, perhaps by incorporating an amount of money in your fee structure to be earmarked for these improvements. If you wish to build a counsellor training course of the quality recognized by BAC criteria, then you must, for example, provide a well-stocked library, or at least arrangements for access to one.

The space at your disposal dictates the size of group you can train. Visibility and audibility are of course extremely important. Since most adult counselling trainees prefer not to sit in lecture theatre-style rows, consider whether your main training rooms can accommodate the 12, 18 or 24 or more people you propose to train. If everyone sits in a circle or horseshoe, is the flipchart visible and your writing readable? Is there a wall or screen on which you can project overheads? Is there sufficient usable space for sticking large sheets of paper on? Is there space for noticeboards, pigeonholes, coat hooks? And is there permission to use space in these ways? Are there sufficient power sockets, tables and any other supporting equipment you may need?

How understanding and helpful are the key staff in your institution? Are deans, department heads, co-tutors, secretaries, technicians, cleaners and all concerned with your environment sympathetic to your needs and aims? Counsellor training, from first advertising through to mailing of brochures, receipt of applications, invitations to interview, myriad correspondence, invoicing, message-taking, photocopying, record-keeping and trouble-shooting, involves a great deal of paperwork which is often processed or assisted by secretarial staff. It is also important that those staff members communicate sensitively with present and potential students, whether in person or on the telephone. Course directors and tutors need to ensure that tasks are understood, accepted and executed efficiently, since things can go seriously wrong when the infrastructure fails. Sometimes messages fail to get through, staff sicknesses may inevitably lead to strain on other staff, and it is therefore important to appreciate that both efficiency and flexibility are necessary. Trainees will not necessarily be forgiving if vital documents go astray, timetables are not notified and things do not run as advertised!

To some extent trainees' acceptance of particular environments is influenced by the nature of the course. More humanistic courses, for example, may require greater space or floor cushions. Psychodynamic courses which demonstrate poor respect for their environment fail to mirror the importance of the counsellor–client relationship and the environmental frame in which it is held. The more cognitive-behavioural courses, however, may be able to refer to the imperfection of the environment as an example of the fact that the world does not conform to our irrational demands for total comfort. Generally speaking, sufficient and appropriate space, furniture, warmth and basic facilities are the bottom line. Most counselling trainees probably do not expect, and may not want, the level of sophisticated facilities you might find in a management training centre, for example. But take care of your training environment. Do not let plants wither, lightbulbs remain unreplaced, floors remain slippery and fire drills go unexplained. Create and maintain as friendly and training-oriented a setting as possible within your resources.

> **Key point**
>
> Survey the advantages and disadvantages of your training venue externally and internally and ensure that you can offer acceptable levels of comfort, safety and learning-supporting accommodation and administrative functions.

5 Discuss and explore any implications of the BAC *Codes of Ethics and Practice* for Trainers and for Counsellors

The course you are running may recruit trainees who are expected to have had previous counsellor training. Even in such cases, however, you cannot afford to make assumptions about trainees' knowledge of professional and ethical issues. It is unfair and unsound to leave to chance trainees' knowledge and expectations regarding the ethical parameters of counselling and counsellor training. It is good practice to introduce trainees formally to the various Codes of Ethics of the British Association for Counselling, or any other such codes you may work to. In the case of the (BAC) *Code of Ethics and Practice for Trainers* (see Appendix 1), we advocate that you spend training time explicitly examining its contents early on in the course. This practice is a valuable organizational aid, since it helps trainees to orientate themselves professionally and to be clear about their relationships with trainers.

The BAC *Code of Ethics and Practice for Trainers* (which we will refer to here as 'the Code') reflects the values of the Code of Ethics and Practice for Counsellors. Counselling is to be viewed as a responsible, professional, disciplined activity which respects the dignity, autonomy and right to self-determination of all clients. Likewise, counsellor training should reflect this respect, even though trainees have certain obligations (such as meeting standards of performance) which counselling clients do not have. Open exploration of the Code with trainees models the clarity and contract-making which they will later be expected to practise with clients. The Code acknowledges that trainees may undergo painful experiences during training which may render them vulnerable, and which should be handled sensitively by both trainers and by other trainees. Trainers are expected by the Code to establish and maintain appropriate boundaries between, for example, the training relationship and friendship. Sexual activity between trainers and trainees is explicitly prohibited. This latter point is not automatically known to trainees and is not invariably observed by all trainers! The purpose of this prohibition, as well as modelling essential boundaries for counsellors, is to ensure that care for, and necessary assessment of trainees is not compromised by relationships which slide into over-intimate pairings. Such relationships are, of course, also extremely divisive within the course, and ultimately unmanageable. Similarly, trainers should not seek any form of emotional gratification from trainees; neither should they slip into treating trainees as clients.

As well as these relationship boundaries, trainers are expected to establish clear boundaries of confidentiality within the training setting. Like confidentiality in counselling, confidentiality in training needs to be negotiated and its limits understood and agreed. A great deal of personal material arises within training, and it is fitting that most of it is considered confidential. However, there may be occasions when a tutor has concerns about particular trainees which call for consultation with other tutors or colleagues. We have mentioned elsewhere the dilemma that might arise should supervisors who are attached to training courses have serious concerns about the competency or ethical behaviour of trainees (see pp. 17 and 107). You need to consider what kind of information may be so important in terms of protecting future clients that you may be prepared to breach confidentiality by discussing trainees' disclosures with other tutors or members of your examining board. You also need to ensure that trainees clearly understand what are the limits to confidentiality.

Further sections of the Code cover the competence of trainers, their responsibilities, their management of training and the routes available for trainees' complaints. Now, it may be evident that this sort of document is in effect a list of guidelines and prohibitions that does not lend itself readily to debate or negotiation, and which may therefore not make for very exciting material. To some extent, this is true. If you set out to read through this document and the Codes for Counsellors and for Counselling Skills Trainers, you are unlikely to provide a stimulating session for your trainees. Think about alternatives, then. One way of presenting the issues is to devise scenarios which illuminate the major ethical points, and have trainees discuss these, role-play them or bring them alive in other ways. Another method is to appoint small groups to study areas of the Codes and find innovative ways of reporting back to the large group. Such exercises can be conducted with humour and imagination. The purpose of covering the material in the Codes is to ensure understanding of boundaries and responsibilities and to set the basic parameters for the duration of the whole course. As we have said, another significant purpose is to raise awareness of the need for counsellors to embody high levels of integrity. Another way of signalling the importance and relevance of the Codes may be to set texts like Masson's (1991) *Against Therapy* which outline cases of abuse by therapists, and insist on ongoing consideration being given to issues of professional clarity and integrity. Consult, too, Bond (1993) for a full treatment of the subject of standards and ethics.

Key point

Explicitly introduce and explore the details contained in the relevant Codes of Ethics and Practice for Counsellors, Trainers of Counsellors and Trainers in Counselling Skills, using whatever exercises may help to enliven and illustrate the subject matter.

Improvements in
Training Methods

6 Acknowledge and respond to the learning needs of adult trainees

Since most counsellor training is aimed at people who have had some previous experience in caring or helping roles, it is generally unlikely that your trainees will not be adults, and often they will be adults of mature age. They may be highly educated students graduating from psychology and related courses, they may be making a transition from certain professions such as teaching or nursing, or they may be mature people who are returning to training and study after many years spent in child-rearing or other occupations. This maturity factor has a great influence on the way in which counselling is taught and the way in which decisions are made within counsellor training courses. Two of the key concepts here are consultation and participation. In other words, as a trainer it is important to listen to what your trainees have to say about their learning preferences and allow them a high degree of discussion and involvement.

A number of courses honour the inner learning resources of their adult trainees to such an extent that they encourage complete or almost complete curriculum-designing by the trainees themselves. Everything within the course may be 'up for grabs' or negotiable, where the core theoretical model promotes a faith in people deciding for themselves, between themselves, without coercion, what they need to learn and how and when they need to learn it. The opposite extreme from this is the dogmatic and didactic position, where everything that will take place in the training is decided in advance by tutors and remains totally non-negotiable. We advocate a position somewhere in the centre ground. We believe there are certain subjects within counselling (for example, professional ethics) and a need for assessment (for example, of skills competency) that are beyond negotiation. However, even within this position, we would encourage debate, exploration and explanation. You might also consider the advantages of learning contracts, whereby you negotiate with trainees what they will undertake actively, and when they will do this (for example, reading up on certain subjects before the lecture). Let us now examine closely some of the issues involved in training adults.

Previous educational experiences

Many of us have known, endured, survived or even flourished in an educational system which may have drilled knowledge into us. Some teachers have believed in teaching by terror, learning by rote and setting examinations which will determine students' destinies, it seemed, once and for all. Many students have felt scarred by such experiences and have avoided education beyond the time when they were compelled to be students. But when people decide they have a vocation for counselling, they realize that training for counselling will involve a return to a learning environment. They may feel excitement at the prospect and be able readily to shake off their associations of learning as a joyless discipline in which they had no say. But they may approach this new learning with trepidation, which can manifest itself in various ways.

Key negative characteristics of the kind of impoverishing educational experiences referred to above are competition between students, fear of the teacher, learning without reference to its emotional impact and avoidance of critical questioning. If students unconsciously bring such attitudes to a counsellor training course, they will probably be very confused, since they will be expected instead to voice their views, to learn collaboratively from each other, to pursue their own interests and to challenge dogmatic statements. It may be that some students, particularly those who have returned to study after years out of the educational system, will need explicit permission to engage in this new learning style; and to have this permission modelled and reinforced.

In addition to offering practical suggestions to students about how they might experiment with learning attitudes, you might decide to demonstrate the explicit or implicit learning theory of the core theoretical model and help trainees to explore it in their academic development. Rational emotive behaviour therapy, for example, generates many examples of how people talk themselves into procrastination and perfectionism, and these examples can be used to stimulate academic coping skills. From a psychodynamic perspective, you might encourage students to examine the concepts of magical thinking and resistance in a similar way.

Learning deficits and obstacles

There may be other effects of previous educational experiences, such as deficits in presenting written and spoken material. Students do not necessarily all come from English language or literature backgrounds, and many are unaware of common academic conventions. If your course is set up not to discriminate arbitrarily against candidates who lack academic sophistication (but who may well possess deep experience of life and excellent interpersonal skills) then it is logical to consider how you can help students to learn and improve the academic skills they will need. You may run a study skills workshop for this purpose, produce specimen essays or handouts outlining academic conventions you expect to see used. The Open University produced such a study guide called *Preparing to Study* (OUP, 1979) which explicitly addresses the subjects of learning from discussion, oral skills, reading skills (including scanning, skimming and conducive environment), notemaking, writing and recording skills (including editing, clarity and accuracy) and library use. Some adult trainees express concern about their ability to retain knowledge, and you may wish to assure them that they will not be called on to memorize chunks of knowledge on the course. Find out what and how much trainees need and help them in the best way you can.

Obstacles to adult learning may include difficulty in stepping outside certain mental habits or attitudes. This could be particularly the case for some older students who may have strongly held views about life in general and about counselling and helping in particular. People who have had previous experience of helping occupations, for example, may bring stubbornly fixed ideas and habits with them. Much counsellor training is about 'unlearning'. Students who have had previous personal therapy or previous training in counselling may expect the training you offer to confirm their own experiences and beliefs, and it may not. It is sometimes the case that certain students consider themselves to be 'deskilled' when, after years of working in a helping or caring role, they are obliged to 'go back to basics' or to have their professional self-image challenged. This can create problems for students but also for trainers, in instances where students with previous relevant experience become highly critical of the trainers' work. Sensitivity in both directions is required to deal with such issues. Sensitivity and flexibility is also required in cases where trainees have family commitments which may sometimes intrude on their commitments to the course. In your course planning, think carefully about the likely make-up of your student intake and consider whether, for example, full-time, part-time continuous study, blocks of study (such as, a certain number of long weekends or 'residentials') or combinations of these are best suited to adults' practical and learning needs. Also consider the issues involved in a minimum (for example, 80 per cent) attendance requirement. Against these considerations, you also need to weigh up the best fit between subject matter and blocks of time devoted to it (for example, it may be effective to practise skills in intensive blocks, but this arrangement may not be so effective for theoretical input).

Learning styles

Honey and Mumford (1982) suggested that there are four main learning styles or preferences found among adult trainees. These are the activist, reflector, theorist and pragmatist. You may or may not find this particular analysis helpful, but we refer to it here as an example of how you might begin to analyse some of the idiosyncratic training needs of your students. Activists are said to be people who are open-minded, ready to try anything, who busily look for things to do, challenges to undertake and new people to meet and talk to. Reflectors are data-gatherers who want to consider information slowly before making decisions, they are receptive, observant and perhaps apparently a little remote. Theorists are perfectionists who are always asking how things fit together, they are serious-minded, avoiding flippancy and they question basic assumptions. Pragmatists wish to test things out, to brainstorm, to get on with things and find solutions. Each of these styles tends to respond better to certain learning environments and tasks. Activists, for example, enjoy short, focused role-plays and the opportunity to try things out. Reflectors like to watch videos and engage in research. Each of the predominant styles is frustrated, according to Honey and Mumford, by tasks which are incongruent with their preferences. Any group of people is likely to contain a mixture of such learning styles and you may benefit from identifying 'who's who' and attempting to offer a variety of learning opportunities. There are limits to trying to please everyone, of course, but there are gains to be made in acknowledging and honouring such human differences.

You will expect and encourage trainees to ask questions, to assert their views and to have a real impact on how the course develops. Borger and Seabourne (1966: 253), acknowledging that 'most adults do not take kindly to having their studies tightly regulated', commend the practice of 'learning to learn'. As they put it, 'one of the most important objectives of formal education must be to enable people to learn *without* detailed guidance, to *extract* whatever is to be gained from situations they find themselves in'. Osborne (1987) refers to 'genuine learning' as opposed to mere 'information acquisition' and suggests that optimal learning is characterized as 'existentially relevant unforgettable experience'. It is especially important for counsellor trainers to clarify the purpose and method of teaching theory, since it should indeed be personally and practically relevant and not divorced from other course components. Also, if you expect trainees themselves to present material and to facilitate a discussion, they need to be trained to do this.

It is unrealistic to think that you can deliver a long lecture, for example, without losing some students' interest. Ample discussion, debate, and creative ways of illustrating concepts must be allowed for (Heron, 1989). Sometimes, perhaps, you must tread a narrow line between student-dictated agendas and your own (or your institution's) agendas. Remember that counsellors are expected to be 'reflective practitioners' (BAC, 1990a) – not necessarily in the particular sense of the 'learning style' referred to above – and not passive, uncritical recipients of lectures and other people's ideas. On graduating from the course, they must be able to think for themselves, to conceptualize client problems and dynamics, to engage with clients in an adult fashion. It is healthy, therefore, if the training they are undergoing honours their unique struggles to make sense of theory and to internalize core conditions and skills, and challenges them vigorously.

Key point

Accept your trainees as adults with a wealth of life experience and skills, as well as individual learning styles, who need to be consulted, challenged and in certain matters nurtured.

7

Use a variety of methods of presenting theoretical material, including lectures, discussion, exercises, handouts and audio-visual aids

We have suggested that any substantial counsellor training inevitably entails a certain amount of theoretical input. At the same time, most adult trainees do not wish to be 'lectured at' and, as has been amply demonstrated, most students have quite a limited attention span for taking in lecture content, which makes it unrealistic to deliver long lectures. In addition, students appreciate a variety of activities, so that relatively short spells of sitting and listening are best interspersed with paired, active discussion and opportunities for movement, interaction and refreshments. These facts have long been recognized and addressed within the management training field (Rae, 1986; Hart, 1991). Counsellor trainers have always recognized the need for creative teaching and facilitating, and the points we make here underline this need and how it can be addressed.

Lectures

While some courses seek to avoid the lecture format altogether, we believe that a certain amount of lecturing has benefits. What are these?

Material which is delivered by trainers, for example on ethical and psychiatric aspects of counselling, may contain essential information which all trainees must learn. As a trainer, you can be sure that you have got across certain core information that you consider so significant that it is not open to negotiation whether trainees attend such lectures. You may supplement your talk with handouts, information made available on a flipchart or on an overhead projector, but the point here is that you satisfy yourself that trainees have been exposed to the material.

Trainers who have a thorough knowledge of their subject can often enliven it in a lecture, clarifying concepts that are found in textbooks, or adding to them, in a way that brings the subject alive for trainees. Written material on specialist theoretical orientations, for example, is sometimes rather dry and jargon-ridden. Spoken exposition of the same material can add colour, illustrations and subtlety. In addition, lectures which allow ample opportunity for questioning and clarification allow trainees access to someone who can explain or reinterpret theory in tailor-made ways, thus ensuring understanding and minimizing misunderstanding.

Some teachers and trainers are gifted speakers whose lectures are in themselves stimulating, inspiring and edifying. Whether such trainers stimulate by their ability to offer spontaneous examples, to breathe imagination into a subject or to invite dialogue, it seems to be the case that certain trainers are highly appreciated for these abilities. Some trainers are simply gifted speakers who are able to bring almost any subject alive with passion, humour and anecdote. As a trainer, you may feel strongly about, and be able to deliver stimulating lectures on, subjects that you are particularly well-informed about. If you wish to strengthen your lecturing skills, consult the literature on public speaking (for example, Smithies, 1987) and seek monitoring and feedback from colleagues.

Discussion

Lectures often form the basis of discussions either during or after their delivery. The dialogical nature of counselling is well reflected in spontaneous discussion among tutors and students. Much, if not most counselling theory is open to debate and opinion, and students are likely to learn with greater enthusiasm and commitment when their active participation is encouraged. However, spontaneous discussion does not always readily occur within lecture time, especially if groups are large. For this reason, it is common practice to organize small group discussions either within or after a long lecture. How is such discussion facilitated?

The simplest method is to ask trainees to form groups of three, four or five and examine critically the theory that has just been explained. They might check with each other whether they think they have understood it, how they feel about it, what they consider its applications may be, and so on. Such discussions may be free, brief explorations with no further expectations. However, trainees need to be trained to do this well.

You may decide on more inventive kinds of discussions, asking groups to form themselves into the different sides of an argument (for example, free will versus determinism) or asking them to form working groups analysing and reporting back on the advantages and disadvantages of certain theoretical positions (for example, of eclecticism). Structured discussion, or task-based discussion, can inject a sense of fun and discovery into a subject that might otherwise be somewhat dry.

You might invite trainees, with or without advanced preparation, to make short presentations on certain subjects or to talk about personal experiences involving some aspects of theory. Trainees with such personal experiences might, for example, share their experiences of working in an alcohol unit or residential care home, personal anecdotes of involvement in stressful occupations, debt management, post-traumatic stress or anorexia. Great care needs to be taken in such cases that students are emotionally strong enough to disclose and discuss such information. The benefit of this approach to making theory personal is, of course, that it brings it alive and adds credibility. Again, trainees need to be helped to do this exercise effectively.

Seminars of small groups of trainees may be organized as an ongoing course component. In seminars of perhaps six trainees there is greater opportunity for everyone to have a say and, if desired, for everyone to present certain chosen topics. Alternatively, seminars may be treated as mini-lectures with multiple discussion points included, the trainer making him- or herself available as a resource rather than standing as a remote authority on traditional counselling psychology subjects. One-to-one tutorials may also be used partly to help trainees to clarify for themselves any problematic aspects of theory.

Exercises

Asking students, after prior preparation, to prepare subjects for presentation is one form of exercise which can enliven theory and hand over greater responsibility to students for their own learning. There are a number of other exercises, which may include the following.

Consider demonstrating theory-in-practice. If you have a slot devoted to some of the fundamentals of collaborative empiricism (the principle in cognitive therapy whereby counsellor and client agree on, examine and solve the client's problem together), or experiential listening (the principle from experiential psychotherapy whereby the counsellor listens and responds with sustained accurate empathy), for example, these ideas are often much better conveyed by demonstration than by 'chalk and talk'. Ask for volunteers from the student group and show in action what it means to engage a client in respectful contract-making or in innovative techniques of advanced empathy. Invite students to attempt similar exercises either in front of the large group or in small groups. Enacting theory in this way is also a form of skills training, of course.

Divide your large group into subgroups and ask each small group to take a particular concept. For example, if you are examining defence mechanisms, you might allocate one or two classical defence mechanisms to each group, giving them the responsibility for reading, researching, discussing and creatively explaining or role-playing for the rest of the large group the meaning and nuances of particular defence mechanisms. You might use a similar method for examining and explaining injunctions, cognitive errors, developmental stages or indeed almost any area of counselling theory.

You might choose to ask trainees individually to research certain theoretical areas and to propose innovative ways of explaining these to the rest of the group. This might be in the form of short essays to be read aloud, presentations of audio- or videotape material or short psychodramas. Alternatively you might suggest that trainees do this in pairs or threes. Ask them, for example, to consider the concept of the organismic valuing process, the false self or the underdog, and to come up with valid explanations. You might also request such exercises to be done on much broader themes, for example to explain dramatically or vividly the essence of psychodynamic counselling or humanistic psychology. As with other examples, students need some help in learning how to do these well.

Handouts

An advantage of handouts, like lectures, is that you can be sure that certain important information has been conveyed. If you prepare the handout yourself, you can vouch for the content and quality of the information. Handouts crystallize theory in note form, or in other succinct ways, for example by the use of diagrams, and can offer essential references. In some cases, and particularly if you are a specialist in your field, your handouts may cover subject areas not currently covered well in existing texts. Using handouts can free time within theoretical sessions for more discussion or exercises. They can be taken away, filed and referred to as necessary. Students obviously appreciate well-prepared handouts which summarize information for them. Trainees attending prestigiously-accommodated counselling courses (for example, managers learning counselling skills in three-day residential units) will expect and appreciate course documents which are presented in a sophisticated format.

The disadvantage of handouts, or their too frequent use, is that they may discourage trainees from doing their own reading, research and thinking. Some trainees may wish to get away with as little work as possible, but more likely is the scenario in which trainees who have very busy lives on top of their training commitments, are naturally tempted to take shortcuts wherever possible to ease their overall stress load. Ironically, particularly full, comprehensive handouts may encourage students not to read and investigate theory sufficiently deeply. Bearing this in mind, you may decide to use handouts sparingly or to issue the kind of handouts which provide only sketches of information which must be fleshed out by further reading and study.

Audio-visual aids

The most commonly used kinds of audio-visual aids in counsellor training are acetates, used with overhead projectors, and video-tapes. Technology which encourages active participation includes tape-recording and video-recording. Posters and wallcharts also offer stimulating visual input. Let us look briefly at some of the advantages and disadvantages of each of these.

Overhead projectors allow you to project various kinds of information in a way that has advantages over simple flipchart presentation. Acetates can be prepared in such a way that a great deal of information (epidemiological statistics, for example) can be shown at a stroke. Professionally designed acetates obviously look impressive and probably carry greater importance in training in management and other prestigious settings. A considerable amount of data can be presented in this way. Information can be left on the projector and referred to during the course of a lecture. It can also be referred back to at will. This form of presentation can be much more manageable than wrestling with large sheets of flipchart paper and unreliable adhesives. Acetates also provide a form of visual relief and focus amid a lot of talk. They can be costly, however, and take time to prepare. Always remember, too, that often only three lines of large writing can be read clearly from the back of a classroom.

Videotapes of counselling demonstrations are probably one of the most popular forms of presentation. Trainees are immensely interested in leading authorities such as Carl Rogers, Fritz Perls, Albert Ellis and others showing exactly how they work. To see the 'celebrity' counsellors or therapists at work is to see theory-in-action as well as mastery-in-action; but it is also to see fallibility, ordinariness and the discrepancies between inflated reputations and everyday skilfulness. As well as seeing the 'masters' at work, videos enable trainees to study actual counselling in practice, whoever appears in the video. If your course has video-making equipment, this provides excellent opportunities for observing oneself and others in action, scrutinizing body language, micro-interventions and progress over time. The medium of videotapes is an excellent one for counsellor training for obvious reasons. Its disadvantages are that it is expensive, whether you buy or hire videos and cameras. The equipment itself is costly and technical assistance may be required, which may also incur extra costs or organizational problems. Suitable rooms are needed, and sufficient time for the various procedures to be gone through. Trainees' self-consciousness or performance anxiety may be an initial problem, although the learning advantages are likely to outweigh the anxieties. When scheduling video sessions, always ensure that there is ample time for subsequent discussion of what has been learned.

Tape-recordings of known counsellors' work or of trainees' work are much more easily made and presented. Audio-technology is relatively cheap and may, of course, be supplied by trainees themselves. Tape-recordings can be made and replayed instantly and thus provide rapid learning opportunities. The use of tape-recording within the course setting may be problematic because of the requirements for space and soundproofing.

Static visual aids in the form of posters and wallcharts are advantageous when you wish to present, for example, rather complicated models of counselling, or aspects of models. Attractively, professionally designed charts can demonstrate the complexities of the three-stage Egan model, the various models of psychological development, the ego states of transactional analysis, and so on. Such material saves you the time involved in repeatedly drawing them yourself, and of course it can be displayed permanently if so desired.

Dramatic audio-visual aids or creative art materials are used by some trainers, particularly those working humanistically with art therapy and other expressive therapies. On certain short workshops on childhood sexual abuse, larger than life-sized dolls are sometimes used to convey dramatically the adult–child size and power discrepancies which are experienced by abused children. The use of such dramatic, impactful images and objects must be carefully organized and overseen, and explanation provided of their theoretical meaning and clinical use, so that they do not become mere theatre.

Key point

Consider the variety of methods that may be used to convey, enliven and summarize theory, strive for a balance of presentational methods and involve trainees actively and creatively in explaining and understanding key concepts.

---

8 Encourage trainees to take responsibility for their own learning

Just as counsellors do not expect to do their clients' work for them, so trainers reflect this in their attitude towards trainees. Although, as we have suggested, there is a certain amount of content that may need to be conveyed to trainees during a course that is not of their choosing, nevertheless there are few aspects of counselling training which cannot lend themselves to active trainee participation. Even more importantly, there are areas of training for which students must be expected to take prime responsibility. Trainers cannot force students to think deeply, read widely and critically, and experiment with counselling methods and ideas in their own lives. Yet they are obliged to attempt to stimulate trainees to want to do these things, thus modelling the sense of empowerment and ownership of change that trainees will later stimulate in their own clients. At the same time, tutors can usefully think in terms of training their students to get the best out of the material, rather than simply leaving them to it.

Reading

It is of course necessary for substantial training courses to be based on core theoretical models and this in turn necessitates core reading material. It is difficult to see how any such course could be conducted without trainees being required to devote considerable time to private study of key texts. It is good practice to issue a reading list at the beginning of the course and/or at the beginning of each module (if the course is modular). A common practice is to refer to essential texts, recommended and background reading. Now, while a great deal of your theoretical and skills sessions may be based closely on core texts, it is probably still necessary for trainees to obtain and study these and other texts in their own time. Some trainers specify in their course brochures or initial training contracts with students that they must expect to devote at least 6, 10 or 20 hours a week to home-based reading and other course assignments. Although there may be no way of checking whether this is adhered to, it does provide an expectation and parameters. As well as set texts, however, it is advisable to encourage students to read widely, critically and specifically in any areas where they have particular interests.

Personal journals

Most courses make it a requirement that students begin a personal journal from the commencement of the course. In this, they are expected to record their observations, feelings, reflections, sense of progress or awareness of difficulties. What is often omitted is instruction or guidance in what to include, how to construct the journal, how long to make it, and so on. You may decide simply to tell students to choose their own methods, content and length, but if so, adhere to this decision. Trainers are divided on whether these journals should be entirely confidential to each trainee, or shared with others, or shown to course tutors. Greater trust and confidentiality is obviously evident in letting trainees take complete responsibility for their journals. However, you may decide to offer guidance as to how journals should or might be composed. You might suggest examples for trainees to emulate or experiment with (for example, Progoff, 1975). You might demonstrate what you consider to be a 'typical' journal entry. It is a good idea to suggest to trainees that they aim to integrate elements of the core model into their journal. Self-analytic reflections would logically reflect psychodynamic orientations, a written expression of one's 'organismic valuing process' would honour the person-centred model, and an action-oriented, three-stage model would reflect on one's work with the Egan model. Note that journals do not necessarily have to be written: if students prefer to make tapes or use other creative means of self-reflection, this is acceptable. The advantage of offering guidance on the construction of journals is that it provides a model of informed responsibility, leaving students in charge of their own learning but with some concrete ideas of how to tackle it.

Individualized projects

A great deal of what goes on in counselling training is group-centred and tutor-facilitated. One way of balancing this, perhaps not in the very beginning but progressively, is to encourage or even require students to undertake certain projects of their own. Ideas for such projects might include:

1 Each trainee chooses a self-help book which has particular applications to his or her own life and personal difficulties. The trainee agrees to read, utilize, review and critique the book as a set assignment.
2 Each trainee negotiates with trainers to research a particular area of counselling theory in which he or she has a special interest. This might include eating disorders, sexual abuse, post-traumatic stress disorder or bereavement. The trainee undertakes to study the subject, present his or her work to the whole group and pass out a handout.
3 Each trainee agrees to visit a certain counselling or coun-selling-related project in the community. This might be an organization such as Relate, MIND, Cruse, a GP's surgery, a careers office and suchlike. The trainee undertakes to interview staff, study agency policies and experiences, to write this up and present it to the whole group.
4 Each trainee agrees to engage in a specific self-management or self-change project. Examples might be devising and imple-menting a plan for giving up smoking, overcoming a social anxiety, overcoming procrastination, learning to paint or learning to drive. This would be written up.

It is also possible, and a good creative and cooperative variation, to ask small groups of trainees to work on projects similar to these, perhaps encouraging each group to allocate mini-tasks to each group member. Introduce and reinforce regularly the concept of counsellor training as an activity that is done in a cooperative learning community. Even when trainees undertake individual assignments they may appreciate the opportunity of calling on their fellow-trainees' support and expertise. They may also experiment with their own learning and obstacles to learning by deliberately undertaking certain pieces of work which they know will be challenging for them. A rather shy student might, for example, read about, research and present the results of his or her study on public-speaking anxiety to the whole group.

Key point

Encourage students to accept responsibility for their own learning in both formal and informal ways, helping them where possible to organize their own projects and teaching them how to get the most out of them.

---

9 Formally and informally invite feedback from trainees and colleagues on your training methods and style

It is unlikely that any trainer would offer a workshop or long course without making some attempt to gain feedback and evaluate reactions to his or her work. Counsellor trainers are particularly likely to be attuned to the reciprocal nature of training and the need for ongoing communication about how clearly information is being received and processed. In so far as the training task resembles the task of counselling, one can speak of the training alliance in the same terms as the therapeutic alliance. It is then necessary to form and maintain effective bonds, goals and tasks in common with trainees. In other words, there must be a certain effective working level of emotional rapport, a shared vision of the ultimate purpose of training and reasonable agreement as to the necessary means of attaining the vision. These factors cannot simply be left to chance; rather, you are advised to exploit every opportunity of fostering them and monitoring their development within the course. Do trainees feel good about the training? Is there reasonable consensus about the course horizons? Are trainees satisfied that the paths and hurdles along the way are helping their progress?

The most direct method of gathering such information is by asking individuals or the whole group. Depending on your style, on how approachable you appear, you may well get candid and constructive feedback. The problem with this approach, however, is that students may not feel free to give honest negative feedback to their assessing tutors in person. Who would tell you, 'I think your lectures are utterly boring', or 'Frankly, I have serious doubts about your competence'? Individually and as a group, students may be wary of incurring your displeasure or of upsetting you. It may of course be easier for students to admit that they cannot understand certain pieces of theoretical input, since difficulties can then be attributed to concepts and their originators rather than to you. As trainers we need to know if we are seriously wide of the mark in what we are delivering or how we are coming across, but we also benefit from *any* feedback on our training. Even if just one trainee, with rather dubious motives for offering negative comments, succeeds in jogging our complacency, reminding us that our trainees are individuals and not an uncritically recipient mass, or causes us to slightly redesign small parts of the syllabus, this is a bonus.

So how do you set about gaining this kind of information? One way, of course, is to use questionnaires. This format allows trainees to comment in detail on various aspects of your training, anonymously if preferred, and it allows you to compare responses. If a majority consider your lectures too long and erudite, then they probably have a point. If only one or two make this criticism, this is still important, but may indicate that you need to modify your lectures somewhat rather than scrapping them altogether! Questionnaires that are sufficiently detailed and clear convey to trainees your respect for their views, and imply that you intend to take seriously and act on the findings. This is empowering for trainees. An example of such questionnaires is given in Appendix 3.

You may also seek feedback informally and formally from your co-tutors. Some courses are structured in such a way that you actually teach or facilitate alongside other trainers. Where this is the case, it is a fairly simple matter to discuss sessions together afterwards, asking for the kind of information you want, and giving it too. On courses where this degree of co-tutoring is not viable, you may arrange for another trainer to sit in on some of your classes in order to observe how you structure the content and discussion, how you engage with trainees, how you vary your input, and so on. For beginning trainers, this may feel very threatening, and we are not advocating an exercise in masochism, but something akin to the observed teaching practice sessions that are required of teachers in mainstream education. An occasional observation session is probably enough. Although practised less often, some trainers tape-record some of their sessions, with the permission of trainees, and take these tapes to a supervisor or consultant for discussion. You may also arrange for a formal assessment of your training by asking a colleague from the counselling field to attend a session, make observations and give you systematic feedback afterwards. Systematic and regular supervision of trainers is not a well-developed field, but certainly many trainers seek out other experienced trainers with whom they discuss training issues in detail. The BAC Code requires trainers to receive some form of regular supervision or monitoring of their work.

Given that the training of counsellor trainers is as yet a poorly developed field in Britain, it is highly likely that you have gained your experience as a trainer from going in at the deep end. Many of us have had little or no formal instruction in how to be effective trainers. Given this state of affairs, trainers may wonder how well their courses, and their own performance on them, compare with other courses and trainers. You may have little or no sense of how to gauge your competency, and it is not unknown for beginning trainers to consider themselves to be 'deskilled' or to fantasize that their performance is vastly inferior to that of their colleagues who are long-established trainers with wonderful reputations. It might be helpful if we try to puncture the myth of the awful and the wonderful trainers. Given the subjectivity of personal taste, interest and learning styles, it seems much more likely that you will get a *variety* of responses to your training methods and style, rather than consensual admiration or condemnation! As Conference Organizer for the BAC Annual Training Conference for four consecutive years, one of us (CF) was privileged to deal with a large number of speakers and workshop leaders, many of whom were extremely well-known, charismatic people. Although it sometimes followed that those with brilliant reputations received brilliant feedback, it was much more broadly the case that a majority of workshop presenters received quite mixed feedback. Take heart, then, from the likelihood that you cannot please everyone or displease everyone all of the time.

What you may benefit from in evaluating your training is to consider the kind of map of competency put forward by Clarkson and Gilbert (1991). Trainers may be practising from a position of unconscious incompetency, conscious incompetency, unconscious competency and conscious competency. This is, of course, a developmental process. You may be able to become aware of your place on this map with or without feedback from other colleagues. The 'incompetency' mentioned here is intended not to label and demoralize trainers but to mark the need for specific improvements. The worst scenario would be if you considered yourself a super-competent, unimprovable trainer, while your students considered you utterly incompetent. But a more subtle problem, mentioned by Clarkson and Gilbert, is that of 'pseudo-competency', which means that you appear objectively to perform competently but feel, subjectively, anxious and under-confident. Such feelings may indicate that you would benefit from supervision of your training, or therapeutic work on your self-image as a trainer, but they may also raise the question of whether training really is a role you should be in. As these authors point out, there is no logic in the idea that experienced counsellors should automatically become trainers and supervisors. Certain personal, emotional, intellectual and organizational skills are required of trainers that are not necessarily required of counsellors. We examine further the taxing demands on trainers and the need for self-care in Section 29.

Key point

Find ways of gaining feedback on your methods and style, from trainees and colleagues, formally and informally, that help you to evaluate and where necessary improve your effectiveness as a trainer.

III Improvements in Skills Training

10 Devise and implement a coherent programme of counselling skills training, based on a clear rationale for the use of these skills and allowing ample opportunities for them to be practised

We take the position that no counsellor training is thorough which omits or minimizes counselling skills. An exception to this is, say, a Master's course which specifies in its entry requirements that trainees should have obtained sufficient counselling skills training elsewhere before beginning the course. Although it is perfectly possible to plan and run a course in counselling theory without experiential practice, we do not believe this equips students to become counselling practitioners. What we cannot be so certain about, however, is the precise skills that you will teach on your course, since this will depend on the theoretical orientation you espouse. There is some debate about how generic or otherwise counselling skills are from model to model. If you train students in cognitive approaches, for example, then you will require them to learn how to elicit information from clients actively, in a style which would be somewhat against the grain for person-centred and psychodynamic counsellors and their trainers. So let us make it clear that the core model must permeate the skills component of your course, both in content and in the manner of teaching.

Having said this, it is hard to imagine how substantial counsellor training courses could avoid paying attention to the core conditions of acceptance, empathy and genuineness, or the fundamental communication skills of active listening, accurate empathy, paraphrasing, summarizing, and so on. Different models make different use of these skills, but none can ignore them altogether. The exception to this is those courses, like certain Master's or other advanced courses, which require students to have already had previous training in such skills. But consider your attitude to, and the demands of your orientation towards, the micro-skills of conscious body language, greetings and signs of attentiveness towards clients; core emotional dispositions; basic counselling or communication skills; and strategic, approach-specific skills. If your model is an Egan-based one, then you will logically demonstrate and foster the learning of the most basic micro-skills before moving on to the skills of helping clients to tell their stories, to prioritize concerns and to become future-oriented. However, if yours is a psychodynamic approach, then you may spend more time on self-awareness exercises designed with issues of the facilitating environment, trust and dependency and other psychodynamic phenomena in mind (Jacobs, 1991). Do not assume that the core skills relating to your model will convey themselves, and be picked up, by chance. Decide on what they are, explain them to students and design your programme to allow for them to be practised.

There are models of counselling which rely more on the concept of an *implicit process* of skill acquisition than on the explicit teaching and learning of particular skills. It is important to point out that too great an emphasis on discrete skills may dislodge this component from others within a course and fail to show that each skill is in reality an integral part of counselling practice. The other extreme, which we are cautioning against here, occurs where there is an assumption that skills are being learned implicitly, when they may not be. Consider the view of Thorne on the person-centred approach: 'the work of the therapist is not essentially concerned with dispensing wisdom or expertise or even with the deploying of skills. It is more to do with embodying values consistently no matter how great the client's confusion, resistance or even hostility' (1989: 64). Thorne and other person-centred counsellors emphasize the importance of the core interpersonal attitudes and may be suspicious of the acquisition of discrete skills and techniques and the danger of counsellors relying on these when they are not grounded in training for the development of these attitudes. A coherent training in the person-centred approach will therefore prioritize the facilitation of the personal growth of the trainee. A training in cognitive therapy, however, would seek to foster good interpersonal skills as one element, but would also stress a need to internalize the skills involved in agenda setting, pacing, guided discovery, application of techniques, homework setting and so on (see Appendix 4).

Accepting that different theoretical models entail different 'approach-specific' skills, you need to design your training programme accordingly, allowing sufficient time to explain, demonstrate and facilitate trainees' practice of these skills. Bear in mind that if you wish to submit your course for BAC course recognition, for example, you will need to show clearly what your skills component consists of. Individual counsellors applying for their own accreditation also need to demonstrate that they have studied and practised skills, as well as theory and other aspects of counselling. Thus, in transactional analysis, for example, it is not enough to teach the theory of self-sabotage, but in addition you need to show how this is applied. Conversely, it may be very attractive to demonstrate vividly the impact of chairwork in Gestalt therapy, but it is a necessary feature of skills training (or so we are arguing here) to explain and discuss the rationale for using such techniques. Existential counselling is sometimes criticized for embodying an attitude towards life rather than having a specific counselling theory or set of skills. The existential counsellor trainer needs to show that this is not the case. In the next section we explore these issues in greater detail.

Whatever your specific approach, you must ensure that skills are not *assumed* to be in existence or assume that they are being learned. You also need to give ample time for their practice. One of the implications of this requirement is that you must have considered seriously the question of the size of your training groups. While straightforward lectures can accommodate almost any number of people, experiential and practical work always has to be conducted on a small scale. We advocate that the maximum staff–student ratio for skills groups is probably one tutor to 12 trainees. One tutor, trying to explain, demonstrate, facilitate and give feedback, will not be able to offer quality skills training, in our view, if the size of the group is in excess of this number. But consider, too, how much time is to be allocated to skills and in what form. Is it two hours a week, ten hours a week, or a number of intensive, residential or non-residential blocks? These decisions interrelate with the issues of theoretical orientation, course funding and overall structure. If you run short courses or workshops which include a skill-acquisition element, the considerations facing you will be very different, but you may still need to address the question of what levels of competencies and skills you are hoping to train people in.

Key point

Decide on what the essential skills are within your core theoretical model, how you will explain them to trainees, and what the implications are for the time to be allocated to them.

---

11 Ensure that trainees understand each specific skill and learn when and when not to use it

Here we argue that counselling attitudes, skills and techniques can and should be broken down into units for the purpose of training. In actual counselling practice, counsellors may not self-consciously choose and monitor one discrete skill after another. Rather, they may often experience themselves as wholly immersed in listening to and responding intuitively to clients' complex problems. Their work may often appear to be messy guesswork on the one hand, or what has been idealized as a performance of dazzling interpersonal skills on the other. We believe that at the main training stage it is imperative that trainees consider, understand, practise and internalize a range of skills *as if* they were discrete. Our argument for this is that it is unlikely that counsellors will ever again devote substantial time to micro-training tasks (unless they engage in further substantial training) and that time spent in this way is an invaluable investment. Encouraging students to examine skills in great detail is a way of establishing an ability to supervise one's own work and to generate critical and creative thinking in relation to it. Furthermore, there is good reason to believe that effective counselling is based on the ability to utilize specific skills (Ivey, 1987; Hill, 1989). It has also been argued that each of the different schools of counselling uses a very different assortment of counselling skills and techniques (Ivey et al., 1980: 87) which trainers should obviously be aware of.

Whatever your orientation, then, you are challenged to

understand what its key attitudes, skills, techniques and strategies are, and how their differential effectiveness may be explained to students. As an interesting example, the core attitudes of person-centred counselling are said to be unconditional positive regard, empathy and genuineness. The person-centred counsellor trainer must have a firm grasp of exactly what these terms mean, how they interrelate, and how each one of them operates therapeutically. Preferably, there should be some research evidence that can be pointed to which validates these attitudes and their associated skills. In the case of empathy, for example, it has been amply demonstrated that this is a key variable in therapeutic outcome (see for example, Barrett-Lennard, 1962). However, it may be obvious to researchers and to you what empathy is and why it is so important, but you still need to ensure that you can explain and demonstrate it in jargon-free terms that trainees will grasp. In the case of empathy, it is not enough to say or convey the idea that empathy is simply unquestionably necessary and that the more of it you generate in sessions, the better. Rather, you need to show *how* empathy is utilized, in which forms, at which times, in order to help clients best. Mearns and Thorne (1988) carefully explain the ingredients and nuances of understanding the client's inner world, accurately conveying different levels of understanding in words and phrases fitting the client's personality, the timing and depth of empathic responses. They also discuss the dangers of false empathy. If yours is an orientation that is somewhat at odds with this, you may disagree with the importance given to empathic skills, but what is important is that all skills are explained clearly and congruently with the overall model being taught.

To continue with the example of empathy, we have said that it is not something to be conveyed arbitrarily. Some commentators suggest that empathy, and particularly basic empathy, is essential for relationship-building in the beginning phase of all counselling. Some argue that it must underpin the entire counselling relationship from beginning to end. Some, of course, argue soundly that practitioners should demonstrate it sensitively and in a timely manner, for example offering advanced accurate empathy that is calculated to 'hit the nail on the head' for the client who is wrestling to find words for newly-found feelings within. However, there are commentators who argue that empathy, which is offered by the counsellor, may sometimes rob the client of the struggle to find his or her own words; it may prematurely supply the client with a warm, parent-substitute figure instead of allowing him or her to feel lost, unloved and not-understood, as was the case when she was a child. Others have argued that accurate empathy, or a preponderance of it, colludes with the client in the irrational belief that he or she must be liked, understood and helped. It is not an uncommon failing of beginning person-centred counsellors that they emphasize the importance of empathic skills to the detriment of the skills involved in offering (challenging) congruent responses. These examples should show that empathy is not an axiomatically effective, all-purpose counselling skill, or set of skills. Encourage your trainees to debate the merits and demerits of the central concepts and skills of the model you are presenting. It is all too easy for trainers to slip into a process of uncritically indoctrinating students into the 'sacred texts and rituals' of their approach. By periodically going back to basics, explaining afresh to each student cohort what is involved in each key skill, and staying abreast of research developments in your approach and in the field generally, you will improve the authenticity and ultimately the effectiveness of your training.

When would you absolutely *not* use empathic skills? When might you deliberately withhold an empathic response? Consider what you would do if a client were telling you about his attraction to little girls. At first, you have been trying to track his narrative closely, using basic empathic responses. You may have tried to enter deeply into his experiential world as he talked about his longings. Gradually you realize that he is telling you about an actual instance of abusing a child. Do you go along with this 'empathically', remaining strictly 'non-judgemental'? (A satirical illustration of just such a travesty was presented by Luke Rhinehart in his novel *The Dice Man*.) We doubt that there are many counsellors who would consider it either therapeutic or ethical to remain in empathic mode in this example, where understanding the client might slide over into collusion. More responsible interventions in this instance would be, perhaps, to challenge, to self-disclose feelings of alarm or concern, and to remind the client of agreements about exceptions to the rule of confidentiality.

This is a rather obvious example of when you would not use certain skills. It is widely acknowledged that the untimely use of psychodynamic interpretations can be ineffective, can alienate the client or even lead to impasses and to clients dropping out from counselling. You would not use confrontation with a client who was already deeply distressed or confused. You would not dispute a client's irrational thinking about loss the day after his wife had died. There are countless examples of the untimely and ill-advised use of particular skills, both crass and subtle (see Robertiello and

Schoenewolf, 1987; Heron, 1991). Give students plenty of examples and opportunities to practise each skill in order to internalize the sense of its potency and limitations.

> **Key point**
>
> Clearly explain each significant skill pertaining to the counselling model you are teaching, check that students really understand your explanations, and generate examples of how and when to use and not use each skill.

12 Demonstrate the use of counselling skills, including examples of good and bad practice by tutors and/or audio-visual materials

Students cannot be expected to know, or to guess at what counselling skills actually look and sound like in practice. Descriptions of skills alone do not adequately convey their use, even when these descriptions include short examples. We consider it essential that students have the opportunity to observe, from the beginning of training, direct examples of counselling skills in use. They will of course see each other in action, but this is quite different from observing experienced practitioners. The main examples of such practitioners will be you, their own trainers. This means that you must be experienced and you must be willing and able to demonstrate the many skills which are to be conveyed and practised on your course. We think this implies, too, that counsellor trainers should themselves have an ongoing caseload of clients which necessitates their keeping their own skills in use.

Having explained to trainees what each skill consists of, and when it is applicable, your task is then to demonstrate in short presentations exactly how each skill or technique is used in context. Do this by asking for volunteers from among trainees. You may decide either to ask for real material, if trainees are willing to share personal concerns in front of your skills group, or to role-play. The advantage of a role-play when you are attempting to demonstrate specific skills is that you can control to some extent the likelihood that the 'client's' material will lend itself to the use of those skills. There is little use in trying to demonstrate confrontational skills if your volunteer client bursts into tears as soon as he or she begins and talks only about delicate, painful personal issues. So consider carefully how you will structure such demonstration exercises and consider in advance what may go wrong. Simple demonstrations of paraphrasing, reflection of content or counsellor self-disclosure may lead to very few problems for trainees acting the part of the client. If you set out, however, to demonstrate the actual use of reflection of feeling, flooding or Gestalt chairwork, then you may be courting a greater risk of arousing strong feelings and anxieties which in turn may become unpredictable, and may overshadow the original purpose of the exercise. On the other hand, demonstrations of this latter kind which turn out well may sometimes make a greater learning impact than other, less vivid skill models.

Let us look now at some possible examples, beginning with a demonstration of good practice in the use of reflection of content.

Client (Trainee): I just don't know whether to move or not. It's a long way to go, Nottingham, and the only person I know there is my son. I'll have to sell my house, and leave my friends behind. It's a big decision.

Counsellor (Trainer): You're wondering whether to move all the way to Nottingham, where your son lives, but you don't know anyone else there, whereas here you have friends. You'll have to sell your house, too, and all these considerations add up to a difficult decision.

You might use the same example to demonstrate poor practice in the use of reflective skills.

Counsellor: You don't want to move to Norwich just to please your son. You like your house, and you'd be better off staying with your friends.

The first example demonstrates an accurate representation of what the client says and quite closely models the principle of neither adding to nor subtracting from what the client says. This skill involves careful listening, understanding, retention and accurate reflection of information, plus a certain deliberate restraint. The phrase 'skilful neglect' has been used of the conscious choice not to interpret or attempt in other ways to challenge or deepen clients' statements.

The second example demonstrates many errors, including sloppy listening, incorrect understanding of facts, arbitrary and incorrect interpretations and unsolicited advice-giving. This is of course an intentionally poor response, designed to show gaffes and lack of skill openly. The purpose of doing this is to make it *obvious* what is wrong so that trainees have a 'negative yardstick' to refer to. But demonstrations like this can also produce laughter and relief, and we believe that humour and lightness is a necessary ingredient in counsellor training. To some extent, too, when you demonstrate poor skills like this, you are showing that you are not afraid to 'make a fool of yourself' in front of trainees, and this can help to lessen trainees' anxieties about their own performance. It has been noted (Ford, 1979) that the modelling of skills consists of the model, the message, and the medium. Ford's 'message' corresponds with what we are here referring to as examples of good and bad practice, and the 'medium' refers to how demonstrations are made (for example, by tutors or videos). As Dryden (1991b) has argued, *coping* models are often preferable to *mastery* models because the former demonstrate 'good enough' ability, while the latter may increase anxiety and negative self-rating on the part of trainees.

It is helpful if you can arrange to have different tutors modelling different skills but there are, of course, limits to how practicable this is. We have discussed the use of video material and its advantage in demonstrating specific skills is that videotapes can be stopped, rewound and replayed, in order to observe certain key features several times. You can use any of the professionally produced video material for this purpose. The well-known *Gloria* tapes showing the work of Carl Rogers, Fritz Perls and Albert Ellis, for example, provide excellent oportunities to observe and critique skilled practitioners in action. Seeing Rogers displaying genuine warmth and empathy is quite different from reading about it, even in his own words. But seeing the 'great masters' at work is also to see that their performances are not flawless or invariably brilliant, and this helps trainees to adjust their idealization of trainers and their possible discounting of their own skilfulness. A number of videos are available for purchase or hire which feature practitioners from different schools demonstrating particular skills, and training videos designed to show examples of good and bad practice have also been made.

Key point

Personally, and by using video material, demonstrate to trainees how counselling skills are executed well and poorly, to ensure that trainees have direct opportunities to observe and understand their range of applications.

---

13 Offer feedback that is informed, timely and encouraging, and ensure that trainees integrate this feedback into subsequent practice

In any substantial training course there will be a great deal of ongoing feedback, both formal and informal, between trainees. Exercises in pairs and threes usually offer ample opportunities for discussion of how well certain skills have been used and improved in counselling role-plays. Observers have the chance to make notes, comment on any errors, missed opportunities or accurate and skilful interventions. Trainees should be taught how to give constructive feedback (that is, feedback, both positive and negative, that encourages the recipient to learn from it and improve his or her performance) and should be encouraged to maintain a helpfully observant, critical attitude to peers throughout the course. However, trainees cannot be expected to have had the length and depth of practical experience that trainers have had; neither can they be expected to be quite as critical or confrontational as trainers, towards each other. (You might consider this in the sense that, to some extent, trainers are paid to be the 'bad object' and to accept the 'projections' that go with this!)

'Informed feedback' implies that trainers responsible for fostering the development of trainees' counselling skills must be very closely involved with skills practice within the course, and must also devote a considerable amount of time to each trainee and his or her development. Ideally, trainers should model each skill to be learned, they should demonstrate it again when necessary, and allow trainees ample opportunity to practise it further before giving them feedback on how well it has been integrated. We repeat the point that skills groups of more than 12 trainees are likely to become unmanageable. A single trainer will not be able to hear, follow and offer constructive and qualitative feedback to each trainee if there is a large group to contend with. Optimally, you will be able to listen to each student practising each skill for an adequate length of time, including time for your feedback and for further observation of the use of that skill when it is again practised (Dryden, 1993). We recognize that in reality it is often not possible systematically to hear and to follow up on each and every student in every session of skills practice. This ideal is probably unattainable and compromises may have to be made. However, we caution against the practice of leaving the detailed acquisition of skills to chance, of *assuming* that trainees will pick up what they need to know, and of tutors formulating loose impressions of trainees' work as a basis for assessment. In reality, trainers' awareness of how well trainees are integrating skills may be a mixture of the systematic and the impressionistic, but it is better to maintain a goal of ongoing systematic observation and assessment.

It is easy to fall into the trap of making occasional pertinent comments to individual students, who appear to understand what point you are making but who subsequently fail altogether to change their approach. For example, you may point out to a student that he or she is using too many questions and is hurrying the client. The student of course agrees with this comment, but nevertheless fails to improve in this respect. Particularly when trainees have strong habits or emotional needs to act in certain ways, they will be resistant to change. How will you follow up on the observations you make? The larger your group is, the more difficult it becomes to keep track of what you have said to each trainee previously. In theory it is possible to keep written records of each student's development in each specific skill, but practically this would entail an enormous amount of detailed record-keeping. You may be blessed with an extraordinary memory for detailed aspects of trainees' practical work, but if not, what will you do? A reasonable compromise seems to be that you try to ensure that you do spend significant amounts of time with each trainee, observing and mentally noting their performance, and allocating times to follow up on their development. A certain amount of pressure may be brought to bear on trainees to improve on their weaker skills but when you point out specific areas of weakness or deficit, avoid unnecessary negativity, be as encouraging as possible, and convey the sense that you will return at a later stage to help each trainee monitor their skill development. Encourage them to identify their own deficits and to take responsibility for improvements. Encourage trainees to help each other address deficits.

In some theoretical and practical orientations the sequence in which counselling skills are learned is not crucial. However, in an approach such as rational emotive behaviour therapy, for example, it is crucial that trainees learn a sequence (Dryden, 1991b). REBT practitioners do not begin disputing clients' irrational beliefs until they have elicited certain focused problems on which to work. Similarly, in all behavioural approaches, it is necessary to conduct accurate assessments and to elicit clear goals before proceeding with a clinical strategy. In the more humanistic and psycho-dynamic models, however, following such an exact sequence is not usually so crucial. You must decide just how important to your training it is to ensure that students become competent in certain skills in a graded manner that can be observed and assessed. It seems likely for all approaches, however, that obvious weaknesses or bad habits are best addressed early on, and eliminated or modified. Also, without keeping track of whether trainees are actually integrating your feedback into their subsequent practice, you will have a weaker basis on which to make formal assessments of their progress.

Key point

Allow sufficient time in skills groups to devote attention to the detailed acquisition of skills by each trainee, ensuring that the feedback you offer is understood and incorporated concretely into trainees' subsequent work.

---

14 Arrange for effective assessment of each trainee's competency in the use of skills

If you are putting on short training workshops or large-scale lectures on subjects of interest to counsellors, you may well not need to be involved in assessment of what participants learn and internalize. Equally, if yours is a course which relies heavily on ongoing self-assessment or peer-assessment, then you may not be concerned with formal assessment of competency. However, here we address mainly the question of tutor-initiated and tutor-made assessments on substantial counsellor training courses. With increasing attention being given to nationally and interprofessionally validated skills, we believe that identification and measurement of such competencies will become an unavoidable aspect of the counsellor trainer's responsibilities (Reid et al., 1992; Russell et al., 1992).

Your promotional literature will have announced clearly what your assessment intentions and criteria are. You will obviously have established policies, either in consultation with trainees or not, as to exactly what will be assessed, how, by whom, when, and with what consequences. It is important to be clear about what elements of the course are assessed and which are not. If you conduct regular tutorials with trainees, for example, let them know that this is a time for them to ask for help, express concerns and offer feedback to you, rather that it being an occasion for covert assessment on your part (if this is indeed the case). Consider what your criteria are for assessing competency in skills particularly. Must trainees show an ability to master every single skill concerned and if so, how will such mastery be assessed? Perhaps your requirements will be 'softer', for example that trainees show an overall ability to understand most skills adequately and largely to avoid obvious or repeated errors. We think it advisable to aim somewhere between brilliance and 'vaguely passable' as the hallmarks of competency. The Cognitive Therapy Scale (see Appendix 4) is an example of clear requirements of what skills are to be assessed and how they are to be assessed within the cognitive therapy tradition. Truax and Carkhuff (1967) established an empathy rating scale which is used by many person-centred trainers. Here we look at some of the ways you may decide to assess students.

Direct observation

We have discussed the need for small skills groups and favourable trainer–trainee ratios to allow for ample observation and feedback. This kind of observation by tutors obviously can include an element of ongoing assessment. You can verbally inform students how well you consider they are progressing. You may even keep a written record of such observations and use these as the basis of a final assessment. It is possible, however, that there will be too much for you to do (explaining, demonstrating, discussing, observing) without the extra demands of formal ongoing assessment. We think that although direct, ongoing, informal observation and feedback is extremely useful and necessary, some system of periodic and/or final assessment is advisable.

As far as we know, it is rare for counsellor trainers to arrange for a formal assessment of an actual or even role-played session, but it is a possibility. There are ethical problems with observation of an actual session, even when this may be conducted from behind a one-way screen. A role-play situation would avoid these ethical problems, but would place an enormous burden of anxiety performance on the trainee acting as the counsellor.

Inferred competency

Although we have misgivings about relying on them, methods of assessing students which depend on indirect evidence of their competency are by no means rare. What we call here inferred competency includes any decisions made about trainees' performance which rest on trainees' own reports of their case material, with process recordings, oral accounts and written descriptions. It might also include evidence gathered informally from supervisors. It is often the case that impressionistic judgements about the probable competency of trainees, based on the manner in which they present their cases, are reasonably accurate. However, it must be noted that some people are gifted articulators who may or may not be as gifted in practice as they are in their self-reports. You may wish to trust all trainees, and we doubt whether many trainees would consciously seek to exaggerate how competently they handle cases, but the undeniable possibility exists that they will be unconsciously selective in their case presentations. Note that this can happen positively or negatively. Trainees with low self-esteem may unconsciously discount their abilities. Two main points must be made to caution against the evidence of trainees' own accounts of their skills: first, they are selective, subjective and unverifiable, and second, they automatically work in favour of more articulate and self-confident trainees and against others. Even so, a certain amount of assessment will always be made on the basis of inference, as well as on the evidence, often impressionistic, of third parties (such as placement supervisors, co-tutors).

Audio- and videotape assessments

There are many advantages to the use of audio- and video-recorded submissions of trainees' work for assessment. It is usually far less likely that they will be able to produce video-recorded examples than audio-recordings, so we will focus here on audiotapes. Students' tapes of their own work are easily made. It may be that if you wish to require tape submissions at certain stages of your course (for example, at the end of a first year, when you are deciding that they are ready to begin working with clients) you will allow trainees to submit a sample of work role-played with a fellow trainee or colleague. When students begin actual counselling, you may decide to ask them to tape-record some or all of their work. Tape-recording is still a contentious subject. We are in favour of it. Carl Rogers pioneered its use for research and counsellors have learned an enormous amount from it. For arguments in its favour and how it can be presented to clients, see Dryden and Feltham (1992). Students who record all their work are in a position to choose tapes for submission which represent the best of their work. Both students and trainers can listen to tapes and gain an accurate understanding of the 'actual content' of sessions that is, we would argue, superior to the selective accounts given orally.

We have both made ample use of tapes in the assessment of trainees. What is required is a clear, audible tape of a full session, or significant part of a session, which demonstrates a range of counsellor interventions. (Implied in this is, of course, the need for a sample of work in which there is a relatively high degree of counsellor activity.) The tape should be accompanied by a full transcript of the session, prefaced by a short account of the client and his or her problems, the stage of counselling, and so on. The trainee should also present a written account of what his or her intentions were in the session, and demonstrate an awareness of what went 'according to plan' and what did not, what might have been done differently and what has been learned from the session. In addition, you need some sort of scale according to which you will rate the performance. It is good practice to share this scale in advance with trainees who are to be assessed.

Key point

Devise a means and system of assessment that is congruent with the course orientation, which is clearly publicized and understood by students, and which lends itself to fair, clear and suitably gradable criteria.

IV Improvements in Delivery of Theory

15 Decide on and represent the core theoretical model comprehensively and encourage students to consider it critically in the light of competing theories and emerging professional developments

It is one of the BAC's criteria for recognized courses that a core theoretical model be presented comprehensively. This means that such courses cannot have a theoretical vacuum at their centre and neither can they consist of myriad bits of theory and diverse aspects of practice masquerading as eclecticism or integrationism. The rationale for this is that there must be a coherent thread running through any substantial counselling course, which helps trainees to make sense of their learning experience. It also means that trainees will study and practise in depth one core approach to counselling rather than attempting to become ill-equipped 'Jacks – or Jills – of all trades'. The generally accepted meaning of core theoretical model is a recognized approach such as the person-centred, psychodynamic, cognitive-behavioural or psychosynthesis, for example. Some take it to mean, more broadly, a humanistic or analytic approach.

But it can also mean an eclectic or integrative approach if that is well defined rather than a loose ragbag of theoretical odds and ends or a few token lectures on a variety of models which students are left to piece together as best they can. A valid eclectic or integrative approach, like other approaches, should define itself clearly. It should demonstrate what assumptions it makes about the nature of human beings. It should contain explanations of how psychological problems occur, how they are perpetuated and how they are changed by counselling. The essential therapeutic interventions of the model must be clearly explained, including references to the way in which these interventions vary purposefully from client to client and from stage to stage of the counselling process. Any discrepancies within the model should be addressed and explained. These concepts should be conveyed clearly to trainees rather than remaining the private or intuitive thoughts of trainers. Like other models, eclectic or integrative models should permeate the course structure as far as possible.

Here is an example of a description of the person-centred model as given in the Jordanhill College (now part of the University of Strathclyde, Glasgow) Counselling Unit's courses brochure:

> The core theoretical model of the Counselling Unit training is the Person Centred approach. Person Centred counselling, developed by Carl Rogers and his associates during the past fifty years, is characterised by certain beliefs and attitudes which serve to distinguish it from both the analytical and behavioural traditions. The person centred philosophy takes an optimistic view of human nature. The counsellor is seen as a person whose essential skill lies in the ability to create a particular kind of relationship with clients within which the client is enabled to discover his or her own resources for moving towards a more satisfying way of being. The counsellor attempts to offer a relationship which by its quality of respect, understanding and openness, makes possible for the client a new appraisal of self and an opportunity for change and development. Central to the therapeutic activity is the practitioner's capacity for and willingness to identify and relinquish prejudice and responses which impede the growth of others through the abuse, however subtle, of personal power.

Such a statement clearly aligns a course with a well established tradition in counselling and succinctly explains some of the central principles. Similar statements may easily be imagined (or found) within the promotional literature of quite different models. What might an eclectic or integrative statement look like?:

> The core theoretical model of this course is a systematic eclecticism which is based on the work of Egan, Ivey, Nelson-Jones, Arnold Lazarus and others. This model is characterized by the belief that human beings are highly complex and that neither counselling practice nor research to date has found conclusive answers to the questions of psychological malaise and remedy. Research has not validated any one approach to helping as being more effective than any other. Our eclectic model builds from the belief, widely shared in the counselling community, that certain fundamental communication skills are necessary to form therapeutic alliances. These skills can be studied, understood and refined in the service of clients. Research and clinical practice can be reflected on to suggest how different skills can best be used with different clients, with different kinds of problems, at different stages of personal change. Our model is well-informed, but it is also pragmatic, seeking to promote active, effective change in clients' lives. We recognize that different clients want and need different, individualized

forms of help. We therefore seek to cultivate counsellors who are highly trained in interpersonal skills, who are able to choose strategies with clients intelligently, and who are responsive to the ethical and economic issues of clients' informed consent and common time-limited constraints.

Having identified and satisfactorily explained the core model, you are faced with the task of presenting its many aspects and ramifications to trainees. Now, it is all too easy to teach a specific approach, especially if you are emotionally very attached to it, as if it is the answer to all personal problems, is unquestionably superior to all other approaches, and must on no account be seriously criticized. Indeed, in some quarters it seems possible that trainees who question the core model risk accusations of resistance and other forms of personal psychopathology. Obviously it is not helpful when trainees deliberately set out to rubbish or undermine the very theory which forms the basis of the course. If this happened, however, it would show rather poor interviewing skills on the part of course staff! But we believe it is healthy and necessary, along with teaching the essentials of the core model, to encourage intelligent debate as to its merits, demerits and relation to other theories. The fundamental question to bear in mind is: why have you chosen to teach this model? What are the values and clinical claims of this model which distinguish it from others? Do you consider that it is simply just as good as any other approach, or that it has some specific theoretical appeal and practical efficacy?

It is useful to give both the 'insider's' view of your model, and the 'outsider's', or in other words the positive and negative views. We think it advisable that you attempt to alert trainees to the latest research bearing on your model and its applications. This may mean that you have to wrestle with unwelcome negative research findings. For example, how will you explain to students a piece of research which claims that the 'effect size' of Gestalt therapy – if that is your core model – is significantly lower than that of several other models? In a different vein, how will you respond if professional developments in the counselling world move towards demanding greater accountability regarding the measured effectiveness of counselling models? If you espouse a long-term, psychodynamic model which is only loosely related to specified client goals, how will you measure effectiveness? If the NHS were to begin employing large numbers of counsellors who could demonstrate competency in short-term counselling, would your model lend itself credibly to a short-term approach? Guard against teaching a model which is so firmly rooted in tradition that it fails to take account of new developments; beware too of the quick-fix models which sometimes fail to live up to their original dramatic promise.

Key point

Be clear about what the core theoretical model is, whether it is a single-theory model or eclectic or integrative in kind, explain it thoroughly to trainees in all its aspects, and encourage critical debate on it.

---

16 Reflect the philosophy of the core model as far as possible throughout the course

The Jordanhill College brochure, mentioned in Section 15, explains what the core model is, and goes on to say:

> This person centred emphasis will be reflected, not simply in the content of the Counselling Unit courses, but also in the relations between staff and students and in the assessment procedures. The belief is that the training will be more effective if the staff offer a relationship which presents challenge but in the context of personal support. The staff themselves have all undertaken lengthy person centred training.

Reflection of the core model throughout the course provides consistency, constant modelling, and ample opportunities for studying the meaning and impact of the model in action. By definition, it also reduces incongruities. It would make little sense to run a person-centred course whose tutors were authoritarian, cold, aloof, and who failed to consult students on matters of importance. Equally, it would make little sense running a course based on cognitive-behavioural principles if the tutors appeared to have no boundaries, set no criteria for assessment, and who talked in vague, global, judgemental terms. Clearly, then, tutors must be committed to the core model and be prepared to exhibit its principles in their own actions and in the way they organize the course. This does not mean, as we have said, that they should be wedded uncritically to every tenet of the model. Interestingly, this raises the question of how far tutors should reflect the core model in their own therapy experiences. You would expect a psychodynamic trainer to have had fairly lengthy psychodynamic therapy, but by the same token you would expect a cognitive-behavioural trainer to have had focused, goal-oriented personal therapy.

But just *how* is a core model to be reflected throughout the course? Consider the various parts of a training course: theory, skills, personal development, client work, supervision. How should these reflect the model? Obviously the theory can and should directly represent the model, its history, development, key figures, rationale, applications, and so on. Section 17 shows in detail the many areas that may be covered by the course's theoretical component. Certain models are relatively light on theory, however, and this poses a special challenge. Many of the humanistic approaches and skills-based approaches may not lend themselves directly to the kind of historically well-developed theory that is to be found in the psychodynamic and behavioural traditions, for example. But even where such models are relatively thinly supported by theory, they still have implicit concepts which can and should be spelled out. Think hard about, and discuss with students, the implicit philosophy in humanistic, holistic approaches and how this is applied throughout the course.

We have discussed many of the issues that arise in the skills component of a course and have pointed out that different models place different emphases on certain skills. A psychodynamic course will reflect in its skills training, perhaps, both the rationale for asking very few questions and the alternative means of eliciting information. A cognitive-behavioural course, however, will reflect in its skills training the rationale for engaging in collaborative enquiry and using Socratic questioning in challenging clients' maladaptive beliefs. Encourage and challenge students to examine and when necessary rephrase or refine their questions, whether these arise in skills practice, community meetings or elsewhere on the course. The skills involved in contracting with clients in transactional analysis should be modelled in other parts of the course (for example, the contracts made for learning between trainers and students) and explained fully in the theoretical component. No course can ensure that every element is permeated with pure, undiluted psychodynamics or Gestalt principles, however, and it would probably be a caricature of the model if it was. It would be truer to say that trainers should *aim* at consistently reflecting the core model throughout the course.

When trainees begin work with clients, you need to think particularly carefully about this consistency issue. If you have been training students in psychodynamic or person-centred counselling principles and skills, for example, it would be incongruent (not to say potentially disastrous) to endorse their working in placements where they will be expected to conform to an established pattern of time-limited, behaviourally-oriented counselling. It would be unwise to place students in agencies where the manager is unsympathetic to particular approaches. If your course runs on cognitive-behavioural principles and your students are expected to gain practical experience of problem-definition, goalsetting and focused pieces of work, then your students may become frustrated or demoralized if they have placements in settings where the clients tend to be so confused or chaotic that they cannot collaborate with such agendas. Similarly, if students are going to be supervised within the placement, it may be very counterproductive if the supervisors are aligned with a model that is incongruent with that of your course. Such possibilities are far from unlikely. We have known cases where confusion has arisen because trainees in placements have been torn between conflicting theoretical orientations. Unfortunately, placements are sometimes hard to come by and compromises may have to be made, but such problems are best anticipated and avoided as far as possible (see Section 24).

Should personal development work and the personal therapy of trainees conform with the core model? There are arguments that slightly variant personal development experiences are beneficial, in that they allow trainees to gain useful perspective on the core model. However, the opposite argument is that by learning one model in theory and experiencing another as recipient, you will become confused. A rule of thumb here is that personal therapy experiences should not be too dissimilar to the core model. Rational emotive behaviour therapy and psychosynthesis, for example, are probably unhelpfully dissimilar. Gestalt and transactional analysis tend to be complementary. A rather different consideration faces you in relation to personal development groups: do you hire facilitators who will mirror the core model, complement it, 'do their own thing', or negotiate with trainees about what they want? On a student-centred course, negotiation and choice is of paramount importance. A course which promotes rational thinking may be better served by a personal development group which challenges trainees' irrational thinking than by a group which promotes, for example, the principles of primal therapy. You must decide on the degrees of consistency, complementarity and challenge which you consider optimal for trainees' development, but decide these issues in an informed manner rather than leaving it to chance.

Key point

Design the course so that the principles of its core model are reflected as consistently as possible across its various components, allowing too for necessary compromises or healthy challenges.

---

17 Ensure that trainees are exposed to relevant theoretical principles of the core model and other models, as well as other salient counselling issues

The unique theories directly relating to the core model clearly need to be explicated on a substantial training course. There are also many other theoretical areas which we believe cannot be overlooked, for a number of reasons. These areas include:

1 The concepts of acquisition and perpetuation of psychological problems, according to the core model.
2 The concept of change and how it is effected according to the core model.
3 Theoretical aspects of other models which complement or challenge your core model.
4 Professional ethics.
5 Social contexts of counselling.
6 Lifespan development.
7 Basic psychiatric knowledge.
8 Research methods and findings.

In addition to these areas, you may wish to consider what importance to place on the differentiation between counselling and related activities, the legal aspects of counselling, organizational and career issues in counselling, philosophical and spiritual aspects, the 'common factors' in successful counselling, history of counselling and psychotherapy, medical aspects (including first aid), and related fields such as psychology, social psychology, social anthropology and sociolinguistics. (In Section 18 we examine theory relating specifically to different client groups and their problems, and to counselling interventions of choice.) In truth, the list could be extended indefinitely if you tried to design a fully comprehensive curriculum. As with other practicalities in counselling training, however, it is likely that you will have to compromise because of limited resources. One of your main resources is time, of course, and the length of any training course is also directly related to the ultimate cost to trainees and therefore to overall market viability.

We will comment briefly on each of the main areas above and the issues which they raise.

1   Acquisition and perpetuation of psychological problems

According to the core model commended on your course, what is the explanation or explanations for people becoming dysfunctional, learning self-defeating behaviour, creating their own personal problems, failing to deal successfully with problems in living, developing psychopathology, and so on? Put differently, why do human beings fail to flourish, or why do they not avoid or know how to overcome life's obstacles before they become unmanageable? At what points in the life cycle do problems tend to develop? Having explained or attempted to explain such phenomena in a way that is congruent with other parts of the core model, give an account of how and why people continue to fail to flourish or to find their own solutions to problems. Your explanation may involve the theories of intrapsychic conflict and the mechanisms of repression, universal irrational thinking and its automatic self-reinforcement, primal pain and neuropsychological gateways and other views. Make these explicit, encourage students to test their credibility and to compare them with competing theories and with personal experience.

2   The concept of change and how it is effected

What is it within the core model that accounts for the potency of the counselling methods espoused? Having explained how presumably stubborn mechanisms of perpetuation hold irrational thinking, life scripts, psychopathology, primal pain or unconscious conflicts in place, deal as explicitly as possible with your model's explanation of how such stubborn phenomena are modified, reframed, overcome or completely transformed. Which factors within the client, which within the client–counsellor relationship, which within the counsellor's techniques, account for the change process? How can you discriminate between personal change as a function of the passage of time and change as a direct result of therapeutic methods? Even if the model you teach contains scant explicit theory of its own that might account for change, you can offer your own, and challenge students to find their own explanations according to the logic of the particular model. Examples of (1) and (2) are given in Dryden (1990).

3 Theoretical aspects of other models which complement or challenge your core model

You might be tempted to present your core model as if it exists in a vacuum, but the reality is that the field of counselling and psychotherapy contains a large number of models, some of which resemble or complement each other and some of which are in obvious conflict. The fact that you present a core model means that you will allocate much more time to its contents than to aspects of other models, but we suggest (and BAC, 1990a, also explicitly requires) that you direct trainees' attention to comparisons with other counselling and therapy approaches. How does a psychodynamic training relate to a training in Freudian or Kleinian psychoanalysis, to intensive short-term dynamic psychotherapy or to micropsychoanalysis? How does it compare with behaviour therapy, cognitive therapy or cognitive-analytic therapy? What are the similarities and outright conflicts with other models? How are these similarities and differences explained, and are they important differences or trivial disputes? In looking into research findings, how do you account for various claims that certain counselling orientations are more effective than others? Particularly if the model you teach rates poorly according to research (see for example, Garfield and Bergin, 1986), will you gloss over this or attempt to address it? The fundamental question to be asked is: what is the justification for this model, over and above uncritical emotional attachment to it?

4   *Professional ethics*

It is unthinkable that any course claiming to train counsellors would omit detailed attention to questions of professional ethics. The BAC has a series of well-thought-out Codes of Ethics and Practice which cover areas of responsibility, management, accountability, competency, confidentiality, boundaries and complaints procedures. As we have made it plain in Section 5, you cannot afford to assume that trainees automatically know the principles of good practice and prohibitions in counselling work. It would, indeed, be unethical to fail to introduce trainees to the Codes and their detailed clauses. Some estimates maintain that 10 per cent of counsellors and psychotherapists have engaged in sexual activity with their clients. A Code of Ethics cannot necessarily prevent this, but we believe that a clear, emphatic introduction to professional ethics and complaints procedures, along with explanations and debate on the effects of various forms of client abuse, will do much to heighten awareness of the need for integrity.

5   *Social contexts of counselling*

'Social contexts' refers to the social systems in which people live and the interrelationship between these and counselling theory and practice. Under this heading come the issues of culture, class, gender, race, sexual orientation, mental health, and the politics and sociology of personal problems. Psychology, on which counselling broadly rests, is dedicated primarily to understanding the individual as if in isolation from his or her social matrix. Critics of counselling and psychotherapy (Newman, 1991; Pilgrim, 1992) often point out that these are largely middle-class activities oriented towards and available mainly to the white middle classes. Counselling is sometimes said to reflect a predominantly white, Western, male view. How does your core model, and your course ethos generally, stand in relation to these matters? Are your course fees, for example, so expensive that they automatically discriminate against working-class, black or disabled candidates? Is the theory of lifespan development and psychopathology it embraces concerned exclusively with the inner world of the individual? Do you take seriously and present to students the statistics relating to unemployment and mental health, for example? Does your course encourage students to investigate the epidemiology of mental distress and the differential availability of counselling and psychotherapy to clients who do not fall within the 'YAVIS' description (young, attractive, verbal, intelligent and successful)? When you deal with social context questions, do you marginalize them within the course or give them central importance?

6 Lifespan development

Does the core model have a clear concept of how human beings develop? If it does, where does it begin and end? Some theories, for example, concentrate on the first few years of life and direct very little attention to mid-life or old age, as if all that is formative happens and is over with at the beginning of life. Humanistic theories like primal therapy and primal integration suggest that individual life and life problems often begin in the womb (if not before). Certain transpersonal theories subscribe to belief in previous incarnations (past lives therapy) and to posthumous survival and forms of karmic self-development. Jung places some emphasis on the second half of life. Where does your model belong within this wide spectrum, and how does it account for any emphasis or bias? John Rowan (in Dryden, 1992) argues that no counsellor training is adequate which fails to address developmental issues from the intra-uterine to the transpersonal.

7 Basic psychiatric knowledge

Counsellors are not psychiatrists and often go to some lengths to disavow all connection with the profession of psychiatry. However, it is not possible in our view to train counsellors responsibly without addressing certain concepts and eventualities which fall under the psychiatric banner. Counsellors must have some way of deciding when a client is seriously mentally ill and outside the scope of their expertise or care. They must then have some idea of where and how to refer such clients on to more suitable facilities. A basic knowledge of the Mental Health Act (1983) is helpful. A basic knowledge of the kinds of medication clients may be using is useful, along with guidelines for trainees as to any counter indications for counselling people who are using medication. Knowledge of the effects of medication and factors involved in withdrawal are also very useful. Your core theoretical model may or may not lend itself sympathetically to the study of psychiatric classifications; behaviour therapy does, and to some extent transactional analysis and psychodynamic counselling do, but person-centred counselling and experiential psychotherapy do not, for example. Even so, consider seriously the implications of omitting such a component from your course, and consider too, as some courses do, the practical wisdom of asking trainees to complete a short psychiatric placement.

8 Research methods and findings

There is some evidence that a majority of counsellors dislike and would rather ignore research (Dryden, 1991b). We believe it is important to challenge this attitude within training. Although you may not wish to promote a 'scientific' model of research, we believe it is essential to introduce the reasons for some form of research in counselling. The humanistic methods of active and participative research, for example, are quite different from typical quantitative research methods, but yield valid data of their own. We suggest that you encourage trainees who will not be learning any rigorous research methods to discuss the perceived problems of research as well as the problems that would arise if the field remained totally unresearched. If we had nothing whatsoever to guide us in the development of counselling, our efforts would be determined entirely by subjective factors. Having debated the perceived problems of research and those inherent in avoiding research, outline some of the main methods, or if necessary coopt a specialist to present a short input. It may also be the case, if yours is a training course in a psychology department, for example, that you are required to run a stringent research component. Be clear about the differences between training students to become competent researchers and training them to become informed consumers of research literature.

Key point

Consider the variety of theoretical contributions that will adequately inform trainees, decide which are crucial to the course, which may be optional, and how these are all presented in relation to the core model.

---

18 Encourage trainees to reflect on the specific needs of client groups, their particular problems and interventions of choice

In this Section our concern is with specialist training and knowledge of specific interventions for certain client problems. There are some in-depth training courses designed with certain client groups in mind, for example students, people with AIDS, people with cancer and people experiencing fertility problems. Most of these courses are short, intensive or of much shorter duration than, for example, BAC recognized courses. (Relate's training in couple counselling is a substantial course, however.) Many such courses are run by specialist agencies for trainees who are already working in those fields or who wish to move into them. A quite different consideration arises when you decide to plan elements of specialist training into a generic course. Guest lecturers with expertise in certain fields may be brought in to complement the knowledge possessed by your core staff team. You may be able to talk about counselling the victims of torture, for example, but you are unlikely, unless fortuitously, to have any in-depth knowledge or experience of the field.

It is obviously not good practice to claim that your course deals in an in-depth manner with specialized topics if this is not the case, or if the tutors really do not have the necessary specialist background. But it is important that any generic training pays attention to the concept of client groups with special needs as well as individual clients with well-defined problems and counselling needs. It would be a poor training which did not alert trainees to the nature of drug addiction, eating disorders and severe depression, for example. At this point, it is necessary to raise the point that different theoretical core models do, of course, differ in their views on specific client problems. If yours is a 'holistic' approach underpinned by the belief that all human problems are interrelated and stem from unconscious conflict or from being out of touch with one's organismic needs, then you may decry or play down the idea that there are distinct client groups and client problems. This is not our own view. We do not go to the extreme of claiming that there is a specific set of skills, interventions and knowledge required for every distinct category of client problem, but we do advocate that some problems are likely to respond well to certain approaches and not to others (Beutler, 1979; Frances et al., 1985). We also advocate that substantial counsellor training courses direct students' attention to such issues, even if the trainers are in disagreement with the notion of specific interventions of choice.

Let us take as an example the problem of excessive and self-destructive drinking. Problem drinking or alcoholism (there are even disputes about the names it may legitimately be called) frequently involves emotional, cognitive, behavioural, social and medical dimensions. The more chronic and intransigent the condition, the more deeply each of these dimensions is likely to be affected and the less amenable the client to straightforward talking therapy. According to Heather and Robertson (1989) problem drinking is not regarded as a disease but as a learned behavioural disorder. The authors are critical of various aetiological and treatment claims, including the psychodynamic and those of Alcoholics Anonymous (AA). They endorse a practical, cognitive-behavioural approach.

Now, if your core model insists that all problems are resolved by lengthy self-examination, script analysis or primal regression, how will you deal with contrary evidence, and how will you present it to students? In our experience, too many trainers dwell too enthusiastically on the wonders and merits of their chosen approach, without due regard for its limitations, for research bearing on specific, stubborn client problems, and for the ethical issues involved. If it were widely acknowledged within the professional counselling community that people with serious drink problems are best helped by AA, confrontational group therapy or social and medical help, then it would be irresponsible to ignore this. At the very least, it behoves trainers to alert students to the salient considerations in working with problem drinkers (for example, that a thorough assessment of consumption levels is necessary, liaison with a GP is called for, contracts for remaining 'dry' may be necessary, and continuing self-sabotaging and manipulative behaviour on the part of the client may well manifest itself). Consider whether your course meets the needs of students and of their future clients in relation to such issues. If you cannot cover this kind of ground in any depth, ensure that trainees know the importance of assessment, familiarity with alternative sources of help, and that they have the wisdom to know when to refer certain clients elsewhere.

What has your core model to say about specific client problems? Are you in a position to teach, for example, psychoanalytic views on depression, perhaps focusing on developmental issues of separation and loss? Can you point to research which validates this approach in practice? Honestly explore the limitations of your core model in theory and practice. As we have said, it seems likely that the more 'holistic' your model, the less it will focus on discrete client problems or instances of psychopathology. In this case, are you asking students and future clients to have blind faith in your model, or does it have explanatory and predictive powers? In other words, what does your model have to say, not only about therapeutic change in general but in particular cases? What is a transactional analysis counsellor to do with a client suffering from post-traumatic stress disorder, or a rational emotive behavioural counsellor with a client whose child has just died? (For an insight into this last question, see Dryden and Hill, 1993.) If your core model does not generate specific views on such issues, then at least encourage trainees to consider them, perhaps undertaking their own assignments in which to research and write up these areas, Bellack and Hersen's (1990) review of comparative treatments is a useful review of some of these matters.

Key point

Be aware of what your course can and cannot offer in relation to specialist subjects, attend to the specific issues which arise in connection with certain clients and client groups, and to how the core model treats these.

Improvements in
Trainees' Personal
Development
Work

19 Encourage trainees to gain experience in personal development work, including the purposeful use of their own personal counselling

It is and has long been a requirement that trainee psychotherapists, particularly of the psychoanalytic tradition, engage in in-depth personal therapy of their own for at least the duration of their training. Counselling, because its training tends to be shorter than that required for psychotherapists, and also because it derives from a number of theoretical sources, has not stressed this requirement to the same extent. However, it is now a requirement that courses wishing to become BAC recognized, for example, provide and/or demand of trainees a certain amount of personal development work. Increasingly, this has come to entail a certain amount of time in personal therapy. (We use the term 'personal therapy' in the same sense as 'personal counselling', but in order to make it clear that we are referring here to the trainee's own experience as a client in counselling.) It is generally accepted that trainees should know what it feels like to find a counsellor, to have counselling and thus be in the client role, and to use the experience to root out significant impediments to practising as a counsellor. What has not been addressed sufficiently in our view is the need to use the personal therapy experience to reflect on client work. We do not consider it fruitful to 'be in therapy' for the sake of it or simply in order to satisfy trainers' requirements.

One of the conundrums of counsellor training is, as we have mentioned, the failure of research to show convincingly that training rather than pre-existing personality factors is responsible for competency (Auerbach and Johnson, 1977). Another is that despite counsellors' and psychotherapists' insistence on placing great subjective value on their experiences of personal therapy and its contribution to their effectiveness as counsellors, there is little evidence to substantiate this (Aveline, 1990). It has also been reported that a significant proportion of trainees have unsatisfactory personal therapy experiences. For these reasons trainers are advised to discuss fully with trainees the purpose of their having their own therapy, the optimal timing and the duration of therapy, and its orientation. Trainees should be as discriminating as possible in their choice of a therapist and they should obviously think hard about what they will be taking to therapy sessions. In some cases there are clear needs for trainees to work on particular personal problems which would present serious obstacles to their effectiveness as counsellors if left unattended or unchanged.

Another, and perhaps the main purpose for personal therapy, is to cross-refer actual work with clients with reflections on one's shortcomings, subtle inner resistances and countertransference reactions generally. In order to do this, trainees must consider the best timing of their personal therapy. On a two-year course, for example, it would not be helpful for trainees to have therapy only in the first year before seeing clients, so that they are left without an opportunity for this personal reflection exercise. (This is supposing that they begin seeing clients in the second year and do not continue their therapy after the first year.) We believe that a good pattern for self-awareness work is to provide personal development groups in a first year and to encourage students to enter personal therapy in a second year.

Elsewhere in this book (pp. 101–9) and in a companion volume (*Developing Counsellor Supervision*) we discuss in detail the use of supervision in the training of counsellors. If your course provides direct supervision you will be offering trainees the opportunity to reflect closely on their first experiences with clients. For many trainees this is a completely new experience and often an unnerving one. A great deal of supervision within training is conducted in groups, and it is possible that some trainees will not feel able or will not get enough time to explore some of their more personal and emotional reactions to clients. This is a primary argument for trainees' personal therapy and their early work with clients to run in tandem. Their personal therapy then allows them space to examine the many subtle feelings that emerge towards clients, as well as giving them the opportunity to offload anxieties about their counselling work which some of them may tend to hide or play down in a supervision group. However, unless you explicitly suggest to trainees that their personal therapy be partly used in this way, the opportunity may be lost.

In some cases, you might consider discussing the length of therapy. If your core model is oriented towards a cognitive-behavioural, skills-based or short-term approach, for example, this would not be well reflected in trainees choosing long-term, unfocused personal therapy for themselves. (Conversely, a psycho-dynamic course would be unlikely to suggest that its trainees engage in short-term, goal-oriented personal therapy.) Another consideration here is money. Depending on how seriously you take the issues of social contexts, you may consider that counsellor training which already discriminates economically against less affluent would-be trainees should not further alienate such potential trainees and counsellors by requiring them to spend a large sum of their own money on long-term personal therapy. For this and other reasons you might consider encouraging trainees to engage in co-counselling and to explore the option of group therapy.

Key point

Think carefully about the actual reasons for trainees having personal therapy, initiate open discussion about these, as well as making recommendations about the kind, length and uses of such personal therapy.

---

20 Initiate a purposeful personal development programme within the course and consider the issues involved

In their *Recognition of Counsellor Training Courses* booklet, the BAC asks that courses seeking to be recognized 'provide regular and systematic approaches to self-awareness work which is congruent with the course rationale'. This self-awareness work is often facilitated by 'personal development groups' which may go under various names and run according to various principles. It means that time is specifically allocated to this work, along with other course components, and that the work is a formal expectation of trainees, although not something that will be assessed. It is not something viewed as happening implicitly within other course elements, supported by a vague argument that 'trainees are encouraged throughout the course to reflect on their own processes and take responsibility for their own risks in developing their self-awareness'. The personal development group is an essential part of any course which seeks to provide all elements of a thorough training as endorsed by the BAC.

Who should run such groups? It is usually argued that these groups should be facilitated by external leaders or facilitators, obviously people who have experience in exactly this kind of work. For an account of the kind of learning required for such roles, see Williams (1992). Trainees need not fear that they are being covertly assessed during groups if the facilitators are non-assessing staff, and they may feel freer to express doubts, anger and troubles relating to the course when they are protected by the physical absence of assessing tutors and by an agreement on confidentiality. That part of the BAC *Code of Ethics and Practice for Trainers* which states that 'the roles of trainee and client must be kept separate by the trainers', may be interpreted as prohibiting course trainers from acting as personal development group facilitators, as it is by one of us (WD). However, some such groups are run by trainers who teach other course components and who do take part in assessment procedures. In some cases this is because the core model may place a certain emphasis on genuineness and self-disclosure, and may seek to dissolve as many divisions (perceived as false or unnecessary) between trainers and trainees as possible. It may also be due to economic constraints. The BAC itself does not interpret its own Code in a manner that definitively excludes course tutors from leading such groups. Bear in mind, however, that if for any reason you plan to merge these roles, you must anticipate the possibility of some very difficult projections and conflicts arising.

How should the groups be arranged? It is likely that trainers will be responsible for hiring the facilitators, although trainees may be consulted on this matter. It is advisable that groups are kept small. A typical number is eight, but compromises may have to be made and groups of up to 12 are not uncommon. Larger groups may be preferred or experimented with, but clearly have different dynamics and offer less time to each trainee. A typical arrangement is that the group members sit in a circle in order to be able to see and address each other clearly, but this may be varied, and your trainees may decide to break into subgroups, to sit on the floor, or try out various alternatives. A typical length of time is an hour and a half on a weekly basis. Some trainers arrange residential groups at various points throughout the course. The advantage of this arrangement is that trainees can get away from the course completely and concentrate on their own issues exclusively and intensively. All such groups should be confidential to group members, but there is an argument for exceptions to this rule (for example, that a trainee whose behaviour in the group causes serious concern about their skill as a counsellor might be discussed with other course tutors, or might be asked to attend a meeting with them). Think carefully, then, about how confidentiality is to be presented in these groups. It is advisable to discuss groundrules clearly at the beginning and to agree a contract for work.

What should happen in the groups? Some groups decide on what shall happen by negotiating the terms with all concerned. A trainee-centred group might decide that apart from having certain time-and-space restrictions, members would prefer that the facilitator 'joins in' fully and does not attempt to 'facilitate'; or they may ask that the facilitator acts as timekeeper and ultimate safety-figure only. Obviously a person-centred course will encourage something of this sort in its personal development groups. Humanistic groups may encourage or even expect a high level of interaction, here-and-now focus, risk-taking and emotional genuineness. Psychodynamic groups have a certain focus on the dynamics of the 'whole group' in relation to the facilitator and to the group's parts (members), on the unfolding of the group's processes over time and negotiation of bonds, tasks and endings (Agazarian and Peters, 1981). Transactional analysis groups may focus on specific pieces of personal work being done by each trainee within the group. The more cognitive-behavioural groups are likely to use group dynamics and relationships to explore the cognitive errors of group members. Groups provide a particularly powerful means of evoking, examining and resolving interpersonal difficulties such as social anxiety and social skill deficits. Since the range of possible group processes is very wide, readers are advised to consult specialist texts within their core model for examples of personal development groups which reflect that model. Also, consult general texts (for example, Aveline and Dryden, 1988) but when you do so, consider what differences, if any, you consider to exist between group therapy and personal development groups.

We give an example of one particular form of group which has been used extensively, particularly by the counselling students participating in the University of Cambridge Department of Continuing Studies' counselling programmes. Resembling an encounter group, but resting on certain disciplined principles of meditation, this kind of group has been established by Anthony Storey as a means of closely examining and studying human behaviour with as few preconceptions as possible. The group is conducted according to the following principles which form the basis of a contract for work:

1 Everyone undertakes to restrict their observations and verbaliz- ations of those observations exclusively to what transpires within the group itself.
2 Everyone undertakes to keep their attention as far as possible entirely within the group and upon each other while the group is in progress.
3 Everyone undertakes to volunteer whatever feelings, thoughts, sensations or other phenomena occur to and within them during the group.
4 Everyone undertakes to be and to remain as truthful as possible for the duration of the group.
5 Everyone undertakes to be responsible for their own feelings, thoughts, contributions and risk-taking within the group, and everyone therefore has equal status.
6 Everyone has the right, particularly when they feel distressed or confused, to ask to withdraw their active participation, and to have that decision respected by the other members.

The purposes of such a group include the heightening of awareness of each other and the limiting of possibilities for 'flight into history' and other defensive escapes. This contract helps participants to observe 'what is' together, rather than speculating on myriad private thoughts from multiple sources. It enables perceptions to be compared and corrected. It reinforces members' attentional, listening and observational skills, as well as the attitudes of empathy, non-judgementalism and genuineness. It challenges everyone to examine their own and others' very subtle body language, interactional patterns, defences, strengths and thresholds. In a great number of ways it mirrors what is likely to happen between counsellor and client and prepares trainees for the interpersonal and idiosyncratic issues arising in each counselling relationship.

One of the complaints sometimes made by trainees about personal development groups is that their purpose is not fully explained or understood. To some extent this may be attributed to certain typical group dynamics (for example, the facilitator is perceived initially as all-knowing and then reacted to with disappointment and hostility), but it is also the responsibility of course directors, trainers and personal development group facilitators themselves to demonstrate the ethical need for informed consent and to answer the training need for coherence and learning opportunities. Trainees have a right to complain if they are being taught a distinct theoretical model and are then thrown into a group which is completely unexplained and baffling to them. Another, highly important issue to anticipate and provide protection against is genuine and incapacitating emotional distress. The purpose of the sixth groundrule in the contract given above is to respect and facilitate trainees' right to declare their own safety boundaries. This is necessary both for trainees themselves and as a model of good practice with clients.

Key point

Consider the many theoretical, ethical, practical and other issues involved in running personal development groups and ensure that trainees understand the purposeful nature of the groups within the course structure.

---

21 Encourage trainees to use examples of their own personal concerns in skills training

The skills component of counsellor training is a necessarily time-consuming element. It is demanding on trainers, who have to concentrate hard on each trainee and their professional development. It is demanding, too, because a certain amount of creativity is called for. It may be clear what skills have to be demonstrated and practised, but finding and managing ways of putting these skills into a meaningful context is not so easy. One of the commonly used means of doing this is role-play. You may type out certain scenarios which are designed to offer specific roles and challenges to the trainees who take the roles in them. An advantage of prepared role-plays is that you can determine a context in which particular skills will be focused on. Another advantage is that you can introduce trainees to scenarios which they probably would not otherwise meet within the training situation (for example, a client who is terminally ill). Yet another advantage is safety. Although many students dislike the artificial and ('phoney') performance-necessitating nature of role-plays, this method tends to be safer than that which requires students to air and work on their own, real, personal concerns.

One of the issues at stake here is genuineness. As Hargie and Gallagher (1992) argue, genuineness may be considered a crucial variable in therapeutic process, and it is to be expected that differences will be detected between genuineness experienced in role-plays and that experienced in real therapeutic sessions. Hargie and Gallagher's research, comparing perceptions of (client-centred) core conditions in real and role-play situations, in fact suggests that the differences are not as would be expected. Counsellors appear, according to this research, to display no less genuineness in role-play than in real situations. (Since these differences were judged by using videotapes of sessions, however, the authors speculate that distortions may arise at the stage of rating performances as they appear in the video material.) We do not yet know where such research may take us, but it seems unlikely that everyone will abandon 'real practice' for role-play on the basis of such research. What we wish to argue here is that the use of trainees' own personal problems and issues for counselling practice is to be recommended for several reasons. These are:

1 The use of actual, personal concerns in skills groups provides fellow trainees with instances of real, unsimulated and sometimes urgent 'material' which challenges them (in the counsellor role) to offer alert, genuine, caring and situation-specific responses.
2 The use of such material effectively prepares students for the reality of work with clients and the real possibility of having to deal with unpredictable client processes.
3 The use of such material sensitizes students to the often raw, emotional texture of much counselling and interpersonal work in general.
4 The use of personal examples helps trainees to form closer working bonds with each other.
5 The use of personal examples prepares trainees for, and complements the work they will be doing on themselves in personal therapy and in personal development groups.
6 The use of trainees' own material constantly reminds them that counselling competency relies heavily on counsellors' levels of personal awareness, openness, robustness and their being in tune with countertransference and the ability to use appropriate self-disclosure.

We think that these arguments outweigh any case that might be put forward for avoiding the use of trainees' own concerns. Every trainee, like every human being, has a rich mine of subjective experiences of problems in living, chronic unhelpful personality traits, social skill deficits, self-doubts, existential questioning and anxiety, and many daily pressures for major and minor life decisions. Some trainees do, however, deny that they have any such problems! More commonly, trainees sometimes claim that there is little they can think of to use in skills practice. This claim may have some truth, but it can also suggest that such trainees have a worrying lack of imagination and insight. One further positive value in asking students to use a great deal of their own material is that it encourages them to learn the process of creative introspection. While some students are very good at the emotional, 'being with' aspects of counselling, they may sometimes lack the more imaginative and critical capacities.

Finally, consider the scheduling and containment of skills groups in which trainees' personal issues are used as a basis for counselling practice. Short exercises of half an hour in which to practise reflection of feeling, for example, may yield significant learning for the 'counsellor' but the 'client' can be left high and dry, or in distress, if such exercises are not sensitively managed. It is good practice to ask trainees to choose, in the client role, personal examples that are mild and manageable whenever possible. Even then, however, it is often the case that material which at first seems innocuous leads to deeper, emotional and upsetting issues. Discuss the possibility that this may happen, elicit reactions to it, and build in safeguards in the form of extended time or opportunities for 'cooling off'. Remember that in instances of distress, trainees' well-being takes precedence over skill training.

Key point

Initiate discussion of the advantages and disadvantages of real and role-play material in counselling skills sessions, encourage use of trainees' own concerns and facilitate respectful safety measures accordingly.

22

Initiate individual projects which require trainees to experiment on themselves with particular techniques, self-help material and other tasks

On many training courses students are asked to keep a record of their experiences of and reflections on training from the very beginning. This is probably the first and most important task assigned to trainees which requires them to accept ownership of their learning. Trainers vary in their views as to whether or not these personal journals should be checked or left entirely within students' hands. It seems reasonable to suppose that highly intimate material should be confidential to each student and that it is a matter of trust that everyone is in fact keeping their journal without having it checked. Beyond this, its real value is in encouraging reflection, in a highly individualized manner, on all that goes on for each student during the training period. Why should students undertake such work?

Personal counselling spans many domains including the intra-psychic, interpersonal and behavioural. Training places great emphasis on interpersonal learning in large and small groups, as well as in dyadic situations. For various reasons, including scarce economic resources, individual attention for trainees in tutorials, for example, tends to be rather a luxury. Trainees obviously undertake a great deal of work themselves, in reading, assignments, client work and supervision. But much of this work is common to all group members or is initiated by trainers or supervised by others.

Where can the autonomy and idiosyncratic proclivities of each trainee be nurtured and exhibited? Individualized projects are perhaps one of the few areas in which this can take place. We argue that omission of this area of development is a serious oversight, since it diminishes respect for individual creativity and hence models poor respect for individual differences, which trainees will obviously need to understand when working with a range of clients. By instigating a system of projects to be created and owned by students, you are acknowledging, too, the broadly humanistic ethos of counselling which values personal knowledge contributions and personal research as well as 'received knowledge'. For examples of students' individual interests and placement experiences presented in essay form, see Noonan and Spurling (1992). For an example of a structure for examining the personal and professional development of the counsellor, see Dryden and Spurling (1989).

Besides personal journals, other methods of encouraging individualized work include bibliotherapy, presentations, community participation and career analysis.

Bibliotherapy

Ask each trainee to select a self-help book which has some bearing on his or her own problems or interests. As an assignment, the trainee should read, analyse and put into practice the suggestions contained in the book and write a review of it which summarizes and critiques its contents with ample reference to its helpfulness for the trainee. The advantage of this kind of project is that the choice of book is left to each trainee, the book provides an opportunity for guided action and for critical analysis, and may encourage the trainee to pursue further reading in his or her chosen 'field'. An alternative method is to ask trainees to review a body of literature on self-change methods, to submit a proposal for a self-change project based on this research (for example, becoming more assertive or more physically fit, or giving up smoking) and then put this into action. Trainees could be asked, in particular, to demonstrate how they applied what they have read to their own problems in a written report of the project.

Presentations

Ask each student to propose an area of study which he or she would like to research and write up with the intention of presenting the results, or a summary of them, to the whole group. Suitable areas might include HIV and AIDS, sexual abuse, post-traumatic stress disorder, employee assistance programmes, counselling in GPs' surgeries, counselling children, European developments in counselling, innovative counselling methods, counselling services for the gay community, counselling artists, telephone counselling, and so on. There is an almost infinite variety of possible such projects, and it is advisable to ask trainees to negotiate their proposals before commencing them. You need to offer guidance on the suitability, quality and quantity of material to be gathered, collated and delivered in presentation form. The creative challenge here is that each trainee must decide on what excites or interests him or her. The practical challenge is that everyone must find concrete examples and data. The intellectual challenge involves a literature search, note-taking, comprehending and condensing of information. The emotional challenge may include the trainee's attachment to the particular subject and his or her performance anxiety in presenting it to the group. This exercise provides excellent multiple challenges and opportunities for individualized learning.

Community participation

We have known students who have established, or played a significant part in establishing, new initiatives in the community. Those students who have a particular 'activist' orientation and interest may wish to explore possibilities for practically and administratively initiating self-help groups, special interest groups, workshops and talks, for example. One student on placement in a mental health agency was given encouragement to research the need for and current provision of facilities for counselling Asian people. Since she spoke several Asian languages, she promoted an experimental service for Asian people which subsequently flourished. Others have organized small-scale community groups for women with eating disorders, women who care for mentally ill family members, art therapy workshops and personal awareness discussion groups. Not all such themes are strictly 'counselling', but they are all counselling-related, they all encourage personal initiative and teach students valuable organizational skills. It is worth noting that one area missing from many training courses is organizational skills, promotional skills and management of private practice (see Falloon, 1992).

Career analysis

A subject presumably close to most people's hearts is what they are going to do with their training when they have completed it. One way of encouraging a disciplined study of this is to ask trainees to compile their CV to date and to add to this accounts of how they first chose a job, what their parents did, what has influenced their career development, what they think impedes their progress and where they would ideally like to get to. You might encourage them to devise a strategic plan for future development, including a time span. You could suggest that they utilize any features of the core model or other models which would assist in their planning or their motivation. An exercise like this has enormous potential for unleashing interest in self-analysis and in helping students concretize their intentions.

Key point

Include as assignments or informal work, individualized projects which encourage each trainee to identify areas of special interest, to learn the rudiments of research methodology, presentational skills and ownership of professional development.

VI Improvements in Trainees' Supervised Work with Clients

23 Specify requirements for trainees undertaking counselling placements, including the need for trainees to see clients who reflect their own experience level

While training courses vary in the amount of practical client work they require from trainees, all substantial courses aiming at professional standards demand a certain number of hours of client work. A typical expectation is that trainees will, during a second or third year of a part-time course, complete a minimum of 100 hours of supervised practice. Trainers must be clear about their mandatory expectations so that trainees know well in advance how to plan this aspect of their work. If 100 hours are required during an academic year, this will mean that trainees need to see on average approximately three clients each week. If trainees have not secured placements by the beginning of the year, and even when they do, experience a typical client 'drop-out' or 'no-show' rate, then they will probably be hard pressed to complete 100 hours by the end of the course. So the first requirement is that trainees understand the importance of advanced planning.

It is not sufficient merely to tell students that they must see three clients a week or find any placement they can. Discussions should take place in advance which clarify what is acceptable and what is not. Is it acceptable, for example, for trainees to set up in private practice while they are still in training? We think not, but we have heard of cases where this has happened. It may be acceptable in instances where a trainee has previous experience and training in other areas or kinds of counselling or therapy and already has an established practice. But some trainees who are either very enthusiastic or naive tend to want to run before they can walk. So you need to make it clear what your guidelines are on this. Another source of confusion arises when trainees ask (or do not ask, but assume that it is permissible) to work with friends or colleagues as clients. If you have covered the BAC *Codes of Ethics and Practice* in detail, the implications of boundaries will have been made clear already. Co-counselling, for example, is not usually considered acceptable as client work. A further source of confusion may arise when trainees are already working with people (for example, in health and community settings) and using counselling skills with them. They may claim that they are 'sort of counselling clients' when in fact, using the BAC Codes as a guide, this is obviously not the case.

What constitutes a legitimate placement? The most suitable tend to be very well established counselling services in which the meaning of counselling is clearly understood, and not confused with advice-giving, guidance or advocacy, for example. Typical such agencies are student counselling services, mental health projects such as MIND, bereavement services, alcohol centres, family, youth and women's centres and other community projects (see Noonan and Spurling, 1992). Some statutory organizations, including hospitals, clinical psychology departments and GPs' surgeries offer counselling placements. Ideally, all such agencies will have established counselling services which include paid counselling staff, suitable accommodation, referral systems and agreed policies on counselling ethics and accountability. A senior practitioner prepared to act as an on-site supervisor is also ideal. At the very least, there should be someone who will be clinically responsible for the clients so that the trainees do not have to shoulder undue responsibility themselves. Many counselling training agencies and institutions have excellent links with organizations offering placements. In some cases, the training body also provides an affiliated centre or clinic in which trainees can practise. If you have such an arrangement, you probably have agreed systems of liaison and an understanding of the kinds of client–counsellor match considered suitable and ethical. It is not appropriate, of course, to match inexperienced counsellors-in-training with exceptionally vulnerable, mentally distressed or 'high risk' clients, for example.

The level of help you give trainees to find suitable placements may reflect how well established your own course is, where it is located, what its core model is and how much time you can devote to such work. Some trainers leave all such arrangements to trainees themselves. We think this is unwise, but it is under-standable and sometimes inevitable that you will have to compromise and you may not be able to spend a great deal of time investigating possible placements. If you are able to do this, then send information on your course to all suitable agencies within a reasonable radius of the course, and follow up with a telephone call or visit. In cases where trainees live at some considerable distance from the course venue, then it is obviously their responsibility to make investigations of their own, but you may be able to furnish them with course documents which legitimize their approaches to various organizations. The ideal case is where each student is placed in an agency whose senior practitioner shares the core theoretical orientation of your course, carefully selects clients whose problems are not so severe as to overwhelm your trainees and willingly liaises with you. Again, this ideal often has to be compromised and students sometimes find themselves in placements where they experience a clash of orientations or blurred boundaries between management and supervision of their work.

Trainees should be encouraged to seek formal interviews with placement staff and to clarify arrangements before accepting the offer of a placement. If possible, trainers should visit the site and meet with staff. Organizational documents should be mutually exchanged and procedures for liaison and evaluation agreed. It is essential that placement staff know the level of training and competency your trainees have reached and that you are willing to supply them with any references they may need to help them decide on how skilful and reliable your trainees are. It is a shared responsibility to ensure that counselling trainees offer a service to their clients that is not a sub-standard one and that clients are informed of trainees' status (Pitts, 1992). You may well need to evaluate trainees exceedingly carefully if you have reason to believe that certain placements will be unusually demanding and that some of your trainees have the requisite level of previous experience or maturity, while others do not.

Key point

Anticipate what advanced planning is necessary to establish or maintain placements in general, what organizational factors to take into account and what the salient features of trainee–client matching are.

24 Establish helpful communication and feedback systems with organizations offering placements

We have noted in Section 23 that certain procedures should be followed when establishing a placement, including the initiating of liaison with placement staff. As we have said, there are both ideal and compromise situations in relation to placements. If your course has a cohort of, say, 24 trainees, then a considerable amount of work may be entailed in simply trying to keep abreast of which students are in which placements. One way of streamlining this is to design a standard form to be sent or handed to the senior manager or supervisor in the placement agency.

What information do you require? For factual and record-keeping purposes you need to note the student's name, the placement supervisor's name, position, qualifications and contact numbers. You need the address and telephone number of the placement site and the dates between which the trainee is working there, as well as times, duties and number of clients seen. You might ask for details of the agency's referral mechanism, their Code of Ethics, whether they are covered by insurance for the trainee's voluntary work with them, and so on. For accountability and evaluation purposes you might need to ask the total number of hours your trainee has seen clients and the number of hours of (individual or group) supervision offered by the agency. You then need an assessment of the trainee's counselling work which may refer to detailed comments plus impressions, or may follow a certain format. You may wish to ask about trainees' assessment skills, ability to work within time-limited constraints, referral skills and awareness of overall client dynamics, depending on your course orientation. You may further ask about trainees' personal qualities, cooperativeness and efficiency. You may ask for minimal data on a specific case, as an example of work. This kind of form is intended to be completed at the end of a placement, but you may need to have, additionally, an initial signed agreement with the agency which formalizes the relationship and specifies any issues relating to liaison, confidentiality or complaints.

Liaison with placement agency staff is a two-way business. They also need to know your expectations, your standards and something about the theoretical orientation and level of the course. It is also their responsibility to protect their clients by ensuring that placement students have a satisfactory level of previous training and a readiness to practise. One of the criticisms levelled at tutors by staff of placement agencies (in this case in the field of social work but no doubt applicable to counselling too) is that training is often too abstract, academic or idealistic (Hugman, 1987). Counsellor trainers prepare their students as well as they can, but there is nothing like sudden confrontation with the reality of a confused or difficult client to make trainees realize that things often do not proceed according to 'theory'. It must be stressed that trainees in their placements are primarily there for the clients' benefit and not in order to validate, for example, psychodynamic or cognitive-behavioural theory. This is one area in which valuable feedback between training course and placement agency should be welcomed.

It may also happen that certain students have unfortunate experiences · in their placements. Sometimes, for example, a number of referrals are promised which do not materialize. Students sometimes find themselves wasting time, arriving at the agency to find they have no clients that afternoon. Alternatively, some students may find themselves overloaded with clients or with the kinds of clients who are obviously beyond their level of competency. In such cases, the immediate responsibility must lie with the student to sort matters out, but there may be occasions when you feel obliged for practical or ethical reasons to intervene or at least to make contact with the agency to help clarify matters. Another issue which sometimes presents itself is that students may become confused when they are supervised both by agency staff and by training supervisors. Differences in theoretical orientation often make their impact on students who may be influenced by conflicting views from different supervisors. If this occurs and is obviously unhelpful for the student, encourage him or her to raise this with both supervisors and to try to resolve it him- or herself. In some cases, different views on certain clients may become critical and severely test the 'problems of partnership' (Woodhouse and Pengelly, 1991). Only when insurmountable obstacles manifest themselves will you need to intervene. In the extreme, you may need to advise a student to terminate a particular placement.

As well as following the development of particular trainees, part of your purpose in maintaining contact with placement agencies is to foster goodwill and future working relations. The better the relationship you have with such organizations, the better are the chances that placements will continue and that they may even expand. In the long term, it is probably more helpful for you and the agency to maintain a good, smooth working relationship in order to ensure mutual benefits.

Key point

Initiate and maintain clear communication with placement agency staff, using suitable means of information-gathering, record-keeping and evaluation and keeping in mind the needs of the agency, its clients, your course and your trainees.

---

25 Ensure that an adequate level and quality of training supervision is provided either within or outside the course and that it forms an integral part of assessment procedures

There is no question about the necessity for trainees to be receiving close supervision of their counselling with clients which takes place during the training period. There are, however, debates about the boundaries of confidentiality and the levels of supervision which are necessary. There are practical issues involved in the question of whether supervision can be offered within the course structure or not. We will examine each of these points in turn.

Ideally, students would receive some mixture of individual and group supervision of their first counselling work. For mainly practical reasons, however, the common pattern is for training courses either to provide small group supervision within the course structure or to instruct trainees to make and account for their own supervision arrangements. The latter option is chosen usually on economic grounds: fees for the course would become astronomically high if trainers tried to include within it the elements of supervision and personal development, for example. Whichever form the supervision takes, you must decide on the nature of the relationship between the supervisors and yourself. If the supervision is directly related to the training you are offering, then we believe you have a logical, compelling need for some communication with supervisors. How can you vouch for trainees' professional development in terms of their actual work with clients if you have no evidence of how they perform with clients? Another issue arises in connection with supervisors' concerns about trainees. If there are any serious or even mild concerns about certain trainees' competency, then their assessing tutors surely need to know about them. How can you in good faith certify that your trainees are competent practitioners if you have no real way of gauging how they work with clients?

If, as we note, students are required to counsel for a minimum of 100 hours under your 'jurisdiction', then what amount of supervision will you require them to have in that time? The BAC's notional minimum supervision requirement is one and a half hours a month. However, the BAC (1990a) suggests that in order to 'maintain the well-being of the student and their clients' supervision should probably be given in the ratio of at least one hour for every eight client hours. The British Psychological Society (BPS, 1993) specifies a one to five ratio. Group supervision is considered adequate provided that the ratio of time and group members allows each student sufficient time to discuss his or her clients. In other words, the amount of time each student has access to within supervision groups should equal the same time he or she would have in adequate individual supervision. One hundred hours of client work being supervised over a period of, say, 30 weeks, demands that each student receives the equivalent of at least (on average) 25 minutes a week. Supervision groups do not have to be weekly (although it is difficult to see how beginning students could be reasonably left unsupervised for longer periods) but they should be held formally and regularly. Each student does not have to secure exactly this notional minimum 25 minutes every week but there should be some means of gauging whether they truly do receive the equivalent over the course of many weeks and months. Note that you must calculate your own figures if your course spans more or less than 30 weeks and your ratio also depends on the size, length and frequency of your supervision groups (if you provide such groups). You are at liberty to require that your students complete more supervision hours than calculated here, but you border on lack of credibility if you provide or require less.

What supervision should consist of is a subject we cover in the companion volume of this book, *Developing Counsellor Supervision*. Here, our concern is primarily what your responsibility is as a trainer. If you are running a substantial course aiming or claiming to train professional, competent counsellors, then you must either provide supervision or require evidence that trainees are receiving it elsewhere. Where the latter is the case, consider what you need to know. You might devise a form similar to that suggested for the staff of placement agencies (see Section 24). You will want to be satisfied that the supervisor has appropriate experience, qualifications and training. Agreements on confidentiality and its limits must be made. You may wish to stipulate that the supervisor shares the core orientation of the course and you may have other special requirements. You also need to consider whether you require feedback from the supervisor during and/or after the mandatory period of supervision. You may need to leave the trainee to make any direct arrangements which require supervisors to perform an assessment function. Some training institutes maintain their own list of supervisors of whom they can approve. Needless to say, negotiations concerning fees, times, and so on, are the responsibility of trainees in this example.

Our preference, wherever possible, is for supervision to be kept largely within the course. This means that supervisors, who are either core staff or sessional staff, are paid by the training body and have a contract with you. It is then reasonable to require certain clear evaluative functions in addition to other supervisory functions. You may wish to hold regular meetings with all supervisors at which formal feedback on each trainee's progress is required. You may specify that you wish supervisors to pay particular attention to certain issues or to work in certain ways. 'How trainees demonstrate their understanding and application of theory' or 'How well students provide the core conditions' may be your main concerns, for example. You may specify that all trainees must regularly tape-record all their counselling and bring their tapes into supervision sessions. Finally, if you are employing training supervisors you will probably require them to assess their supervisees formally at the end of the year. In this case, clearly there is an integral relationship between supervision and other parts of course assessment.

Key point

Determine suitable arrangements for training supervision, including adequate hours, regular sessions and matching orientation, and decide on the kind of assessment input you require from supervisors.

VII Improvements in Interpersonal Dynamics

26 Establish and maintain a respectful but challenging climate for interpersonal learning

Course literature, the core model, the climate of interviews and the first day or days of the course, combine to create impressions on trainees that may become helpful or unhelpful, fixed or flexible attitudes. Therapeutic alliance (and by implication, training alliance) theory predicts that a poor and uncorrected beginning alliance between counsellor and client (or trainers and trainees) will probably lead to poor outcome or to clients ending counselling (or trainees dropping out of training) prematurely. In the 'chaos theory' of physics, the concept of 'sensitive dependence on initial conditions' suggests that subtle originating factors permeate future growth. On a training course, it is likely that the many initial conditions which constitute trainees' experiences and perceptions, individually and collectively, will dictate the overall levels of commitment, creativity, cohesion, enjoyment and support (or otherwise) which permeate the course ethos. Consider, then, what impressions you create on trainees consciously and inadvertently, from the beginning.

Do you deliberately give trainees a tough time at the interview stage in order to convey a certain impression of yourself and the course? What anticipations do you hope to create or elicit in trainees? Consider some of the possibilities:

'This is a tough, no-nonsense training and we only want the best people.'
'This is a warm, caring community in which we will all be supporting and loving towards each other.'
'This is a kind of family in which everyone's behaviour in all its conscious and unconscious aspects will be under the microscope.'
'This is a friendly, supportive place as long as you toe the line.'

What sign might hang over the door of *your* training institute? 'Explorers and risk-takers welcome here'? or 'Please remove your shoes and proceed quietly'? The sense of anticipation you hope to create or which creates itself in spite of you, depends on many ingredients. The personalities of the course director, head of department and other tutors obviously makes its mark. Are you the guru, professor or high priest, or are you the inscrutable analyst or humble fellow traveller? Do you wish to project an image of seriousness, enquiry, professionalism or fun? You may see yourself as open to various modes of behaviour but as essentially committed to professional values according to person-centred, psychodynamic or eclectic principles, for example. All counsellor trainers will be aware that each trainee will initially make various projections, entertaining hopes and fantasies and looking for leadership or nurturance. Indeed, the training group as interested, willing students and as idiosyncratic learners and personalities resembles the distinction between the 'visible and invisible group' – that is, between overt and covert factors (Agazarian and Peters, 1981).

Individual and group processes are constantly in play between trainees and tutors. However, the core model (which presumably resonates with and in some sense is an extension of the trainers' personalities and interests) also affects the course ethos. A training in rational emotive behaviour therapy is unlikely to pamper trainees, whereas a person-centred training is likely to offer a good deal of supportive warmth. Holiday and termly breaks may be regarded as of great significance by psychodynamic trainers but as a simple matter of fact by behavioural trainers. It would be a caricature to suggest that the core model really does permeate every aspect of the course, but it obviously will affect the interpersonal climate to a considerable extent.

Apart from projecting your own personality and the characteristics of the core model, how will you consciously decide to structure the climate of the course? If you decide to 'just let it happen', you are encouraging an 'organic process', perhaps a faith in self-regulation. Many trainers, however, prefer to offer certain initiatory structures to encourage or allow students to feel safe, to get to know each other, to explore their anxieties and to familiarize themselves with the environment. One intensive method of getting to know each other is the residential which is sometimes held at the beginning of a course and acts as an ice-breaker and seed for further group cohesion and norm-setting. It is important at the outset to discuss confidentiality, punctuality, classroom etiquette (such as, no smoking or eating during sessions, no conversational asides) and issues of responsibility. You may agree that no one is forced to speak when they choose not to, that no one claims to speak for anyone but themselves, and so on.

Some trainers favour certain exercises and games to facilitate introductions and ice-breaking. For example, with all students sitting in a circle, you ask them to talk in pairs and then subsequently to report back to the whole group what their partners have said about themselves. Alternatively, you ask the first person to say their name, the second person to repeat that name and add their own, the third person to repeat the last two names, adding their own, and so on. This exercise facilitates name learning, can be fun and anxiety inducing! Another exercise involves asking each student to throw a ball to another student, shouting the name of the intended catcher as they do so. Inskipp (1986) lists many such 'warm-up' exercises. Remember, too, that you may choose to utilize certain exercises or 'rituals' to mark the end of a course, including exercises in summarizing each student's learning and growth, farewell residentials, informal parties and formal graduation ceremonies. Exactly which games or exercises you use (or whether you use them at all) depends on the core orientation and on your own style and personality as a trainer. Remember that some trainees and some trainers like 'formal fun' while others prefer naturalistic interpersonal learning.

Key point

Consider the effect and importance of trainees' earliest experiences of the course and whether you will actively or permissively encourage certain interpersonal attitudes and norms to develop.

---

27 Organize regular community meetings

Depending on the size of your course, trainees may be divided into subgroups for certain activities, especially the skills and personal development groups. You may have a very tight schedule, trying to maximize course content within certain fixed hours. For this reason it can be tempting to 'forget' to hold regular meetings which all trainees can attend. Whether or not you are intending to design a course to be submitted for BAC recognition (whose criteria include regular community meetings) you are advised not to avoid holding such meetings. What they are called may not be crucial (for example, student forum, staff–student meeting, whole-group meeting, get-together) but it is important that students know their purpose. We look first at some of the functions of these meetings.

Group cohesion

Yours may be a whole group of 10, 18 or 24 students, or even more. Whatever its size, you will know that all groups have dynamics which, attended to or not, have considerable power and which exert various influences on their members and others over the course of time. The larger the group, the more potential there is for anonymity, loss of contact and bonding, destructive sub-grouping, rumours, misinformation and other tensions. The smaller the group, the more likely it is that intimacy will increase, along with the danger of dysfunctional closeness and dependency. In all groups alliances form which can threaten the cohesion of the whole group. These may be simply very close friendships or discontented subgroups. Sometimes, too, difficult and ongoing conflicts develop between various course members or even between tutors and group members. Most trainee groups lose a certain proportion of members who choose to drop out or who are obliged to leave because their performance is seriously below standard. Such ruptures are often experienced negatively by remaining trainees and may lead to rumours and unhelpful dynamics. These negative possibilities are best addressed openly in whole-group meetings where, sensitively handled, there is a chance for both real and 'projective' hurts, misinformation and conflicts to be resolved. More positively, community meetings can be used to celebrate any good news that members bring and any group achievements, such as everyone passing their first year!

Learning opportunities

We have already discussed the vast opportunities which exist in groups for self-help and reciprocal support. In designated community meetings it is possible to foster a sense of trust which may allow trainees to express individual needs, objections and observations. Students who experience anxiety in speaking in front of a large group may feel able to take such risks and learn to overcome their anxiety. Students who wish to learn the skills involved in organization, may offer to take over certain group functions (for example, taking minutes, arranging shared catering projects, chairing a student representative committee). Students may bid for time to express individual needs or you may invite the whole group to find its own ways of making decisions about common and individual learning needs. Although it is usual (and usually necessary) for trainers to be present at community meetings, it can also be fruitful to offer students the opportunity to meet without you in order to taste genuine democracy! One way of not dominating the meeting (intentionally or unintentionally) is to take a back seat, both literally and figuratively.

Administration

The community meeting will probably be the only time when it is possible to get everyone together to make announcements. You may need to hand out certain course documents, timetables and amendments to timetables. Schedules have to be changed and updated from time to time. Trainees have to be notified of any changes in course requirements, fees or other matters. There are frequently small news items, such as the fact that the canteen is closed for renovations or a guest lecturer has had to cancel a lecture, and you may simply want to announce these. Of more gravity are the occasions when you have to discuss forthcoming assignments or examinations and their results. Much of this information cannot be entrusted to a notice on a noticeboard. Because you need to get this information across, you have to give some sort of priority to it within community meetings, unless your course has the luxury of sufficient time to have both administrative and group-dynamic meetings.

It can be profitable to explore the possible uses and meanings of community meetings before actually scheduling and establishing an unquestioned tradition. You might use exercises to encourage small group discussions on how the whole group meeting is perceived, who the leaders (appointed or otherwise) appear to be and who the 'silent ones' are. Discussions may also centre on what the perceived overt tasks are and what the covert dynamics may be. As well as analysing meetings in the beginning and applying 'dynamic' concepts, consider more pragmatic analyses, such as those put forward by Haynes (1988). If you think it useful, employ the kinds of questionnaires advocated by Haynes, which seek to rate, for example, effective meeting-leadership and effective meeting-participation. These challenge all concerned to examine issues from their punctuality to their agenda-raising. Also consider how much value you place on these meetings and therefore what attitude you adopt towards them and how much time you allocate for them.

Key point

Initiate a system of built-in community meetings which allow for group issues to surface and receive open attention, for individuals to use constructively and for essential administrative communication.

---

28   **Deal with any personal conflicts that emerge between trainees themselves and/or between trainees and tutors and, where helpful, explicitly refer to such dynamics and help trainees to learn from them**

A cohort of counselling trainees is like any other group of people who spend a lot of time together. Intimacy increases, bonds form and a common task is pursued. At the same time, subgroupings exclude others, people can get on each other's nerves and divisions in the group may fester and widen. A certain degree of this may be inevitable and containable but it is also possible that tensions will erupt and threaten group cohesion. If you have held meetings where the topics of group cohesion and opportunities for learning from each other have been discussed, this can set up a helpful anticipation of open communication instead of covert, destructive dynamics. Even so, it is not possible to *make* trainees expose interpersonal conflicts and resentments.

It also happens sometimes that personality conflicts and mis-understandings arise between particular students and trainers. Powerful, irrational, destructive and occasionally unresolvable transferences and countertransferences do arise between trainers and students, or more accurately between a particular trainer and student. The fact that in some sense trainers do wield greater power (for example, the power of assessment) means that they may unconsciously abuse that power. In relation to particular students, on occasions when they feel especially threatened or under stress, or because of certain blind spots, trainers may find themselves unable to act objectively towards certain students. We think it is important that you acknowledge this as something any trainer may be faced with. Interpersonal dynamics of this kind may be further distorted at times by issues of gender, race and other differences. For example, if you are a male trainer and find yourself frequently challenged by a female trainee with exceptionally strong views on feminism, how will you react? You are obliged by the BAC *Code of Ethics and Practice for Trainers* to 'recognize the value and dignity of trainees irrespective of origin, status, gender, sexual orientation and age'. So if a woman trainee asserts that she does not feel respected by you, will you become defensive, will you devote a great deal of time to trying to resolve the difference in views or will you become autocratic?

'Simple' personality clashes are one thing, but how will you handle it if you are accused of acting unfairly towards a trainee by, for example, marking down an assignment? Fair discussion about the assignment may result in acceptance and changes on either side, but what if it does not? This is an instance where you need to confer with co-tutors in order to check whether you do indeed have any hidden bias towards certain course members. But it is also a suitable case for referring matters to the external examiner and asking for a second or third opinion. (It is, of course, good practice to refer a sample of all significant pieces of trainees' work to an external examiner for feedback on fair standards.) We have known and been involved in cases which prove to be very difficult between a trainer and trainee. The trainer must uphold certain standards and ultimately may have to fail a trainee altogether when his or her work is not judged to be adequate. Even when there is additional input supporting the trainer's judgement, some trainees still obviously feel unfairly treated.

Whenever it is at all possible, deal with incipient conflicts before they escalate into major rows or rifts. One way to do this is to take the opportunity to bring up the matter in a community meeting, or to encourage the student concerned to do so. Depending on your core model and the availability of time, you may be able to link such conflicts and their analysis with theoretical or skills items. It is also a good idea to raise at an early stage the problem of transference and countertransference and of client–counsellor match. Illustrate this by inviting trainees to consider their feelings about each other and about you. Ask them whether they notice any small irritations or major bad feelings about anyone on the course. They may commit their observations to paper or note them mentally. Then ask them to analyse, by using columns, the objective and subjective features of these conflictual feelings. What might be real and what might be projected in either direction? What precedents do these feelings have in their lives? What stops them from raising these observations as discussions with the people concerned? What investment might they have in maintaining these conflicts rather than resolving or dropping them? If this is done early in the course, it may be possible to encourage open exploration of rifts and hurts before they develop into ugly or irreversible proportions. It is important to convey the parallel phenomena between client–counsellor relations and trainee–trainee and trainee–trainer relations.

Conflicts may also be of a far 'hotter' or seductive nature, for example erotic transference and countertransference between trainer and trainees. The Code makes it clear what is and what is not acceptable *behaviour* but cannot help you or your trainees when it is only strong erotic *feelings* which are involved, except to demarcate the absolute boundary. Of course it is also possible that course members may become intimately and sexually involved with each other in ways which cause repercussions within the course. Can you or should you forbid this from happening? It is usually thought not to be a healthy development but obviously it cannot be prevented. Again, it can be very useful to raise this as a discussion point early on in the course. What are trainees' views on such possibilities? Should there by any groundrules laid down by students themselves to cover such eventualities?

Key point

Recognize that different kinds of conflicts may very well arise between trainees themselves and between trainees and trainers and consider the usefulness of anticipating these by initiating discussions on this theme.

VIII

Improvements in Trainers' Self-care and Working Relationships

29 Take care of your own psychological and physical health needs and personal welfare generally

As a trainer you will already know or have some idea of how taxing the work can be. Consider the many pressures to which you may be subjected.

Administration

Planning any training course, from a one-day workshop to a lengthy training, involves inevitable hours of organizing, decision-making, paperwork, meetings, phone calls, letters, filing, negotiations with printers, advertisers and venue staff, keeping track of course documents, individual student progress reports, and a great deal of documentation besides.

Economics

If you are responsible for planning and implementing courses, you know that you must juggle finances carefully and perhaps incessantly. From your initial marketing and fee structuring, through to dealing with an inevitable element of student dropouts and unforeseeable drains on your budget, you may be constantly balancing, or trying to balance accounts. You may be answerable to others within an institution or your very livelihood may depend on maintaining a healthy economic state of affairs. Other trainers may be dependent on how well you manage the course finances. At the personal level, your commitment to the course may be only one part of your total work portfolio, and you may be stretched in terms of juggling what you earn in several different places.

Time

The time you actually spend on the training site with trainees may be just the tip of the iceberg. Curriculum design, communication with other tutors, lesson preparation, marking and studying may take as much, if not more time than the face-to-face training. Interviewing and holding meetings takes considerable time. Additionally, you are of course expected to maintain a counselling caseload, to be supervised and generally to maintain your professional skills. All this takes time.

Interpersonal factors

There is something extraordinarily taxing about being a trainer, especially in this field. As well as the administrative, intellectual and practical demands of your course, you face ongoing emotional pressures. Trainees generally may expect a lot of you (to be an excellent trainer, a wise person, a fair judge, a caring professional, a listening ear, etc.) and particular trainees may ask for or need extra attention. You may well receive all sorts of positive and negative projections. Trainees, co-tutors and other staff connected with the course may have particular expectations of you and you will not always live up to these. Conflicts of one kind or another are almost inevitable. Counsellors and therapists are not immune to these pressures (Guy, 1987).

Creativity

As well as preparing material for classes, you have to present it in as informed and interesting a manner as possible, and not just once or now and then, but every week, perhaps. Can you be innovative with old material, are you sufficiently charismatic, humorous, and so on, to hold students' interest and respect? Constant subject preparation can become tiring and you need to find a way to handle it before you become exhausted and jaded.

Professionalism

You have to maintain your counselling caseload, be supervised, ensure that you engage in ongoing professional development and that you maintain high standards of work. You are accountable to colleagues and held up as a model to trainees. You may be called on to make conference presentations, conduct workshops and write articles. Very often such work is either unremunerated or poorly paid, and still time-consuming.

Work—home relations

Most trainers would agree that counselling, training and almost total immersion in the world of counselling is unhealthy and counterproductive. Yet it is somewhat in the nature of counselling and training that it invades the home. Private practice in counselling is the obvious example, where clients may physically enter your home and a room is given over to your work. It is difficult as a trainer to make a complete separation between work and home. Phone calls and answering machine messages make their demands. Your family may well be affected by the ethos and influence of your work (Maeder, 1990).

Taken together, and added to the fact that most counselling and training is rather sedentary and demands intensive concentration, this collection of pressures must be dealt with seriously. Even allowing for the possibility that you love the work and have supportive colleagues and family, the accumulation of stress cannot be overlooked. How will you deal with it? (Unfortunately, you may also be looked upon as a model of how well a counsellor manages, or fails to manage, their own stress!)

Many counsellors and trainers make a point of managing time so that there is at least one day of the week that is 'sacred', that may be devoted to family life or recreational interests. It can be so tempting to spend every spare moment reading, planning, writing and marking, that you fail to realize how it has taken over your life. At the very least, then, demarcate an evening, a half-day, or a day that is a counselling-free zone. If possible, do something that is active to counterbalance the relative physical passivity of training. Do something that requires little or no mental effort, or an entirely different kind of mental application. Some counsellors take up jogging, swimming, yoga or other forms of exercise which take care of and energize the body. Some engage in meditation or massage to replenish the resources of the mind and body. Many, of course, engage in ongoing personal therapy where the trials and tribulations of being a trainer may to some extent be offloaded. Supervision is, of course, an invaluable support, provided that you guard against using even this as a form of self-punishing, perfectionistic agenda. (Remember that supervision has a restorative function.) If and when the pressures of training become very heavy, be sure to find someone or some opportunity to offload emotionally or to deal with the pressure.

As far as we know, no one has conducted research into the pressures experienced by counsellor trainers, or into the question of whether the 'natural life' of the trainer has certain limits. It seems inevitable that no trainer will be always on top of the world, always creative and effective (or always financially healthy!). With so many expectations projected on to you, there may be a temptation to play the part of the ever-competent or ever-nurturing trainer. Proctor (1991) details some of the roles into which one can easily fall. Protect yourself by being yourself and by turning to good friends and colleagues to air any self-doubts or problems and for feedback. Ultimately, bear in mind the need for balance in your life and career, and remind yourself that your psychological health depends more on self-acceptance than on your own or others' rating of your performance as a trainer.

Key point

Consider the many pressures to which trainers are subject, be aware of how you respond to and manage these, and ensure you introduce necessary balancing factors into your life.

---

30   Establish and maintain good working and supportive relationships with co-tutors and other course personnel

Although trainers delivering short courses and workshops often work alone, few counsellor training courses are run single-handedly. It is not good practice because it does not allow students variety of input or balance of views and assessment checks. It is also exhausting and unrealistic for one trainer to attempt to teach every area of the syllabus with authority and creativity.

Additionally, as we have indicated, it is not possible for one tutor to give adequate attention and feedback to students on their skill development if the group exceeds 12. The BAC requires courses making submissions for its course recognition procedure to have at least two core members of training staff (and more in proportion to the size of the student intake), who should be of accreditation-standard experience and qualifications themselves. They should also be practising counsellors. These are minimum requirements and an expectation exists that in fact such staff will be highly active members of the counselling profession (for example, engaged in supervision of counsellors, committee membership, research, writing, conference speaking, etc.). Core staff should have the same or a similar theoretical and clinical orientation, or in the case of an integrative or eclectic course should have a similar and clear understanding of the philosophy underpinning the course (see Section 15).

Trainers find themselves together in a variety of ways. If you work in an academic setting you may have several full-time or part-time colleagues who are in some sort of hierarchical relationship with you. In this or other settings, there may be some staff who have worked in the institution for years and who wield great influence because of their long association. You may work with charismatic founders of certain approaches to counselling. You yourself may be a course director with large responsibilities or a sessional trainer within a large organization. Perhaps you have simply banded together with an old friend or a fellow counsellor from the same training institute and you have decided to build a counselling training course or centre. You may be part of a cooperative, egalitarian venture or a hierarchical establishment. You may be paid regardless of the size of the enrolment or your very livelihood may depend on (or fall with) the size of each intake. There are some training institutes whose tutors are married to each other or in other ways intimately linked. Your organization may have grown organically and on a small scale or it may be a large-scale operation with a stringent equal opportunities policy for recruiting staff.

It is difficult to make recommendations for how co-tutors might conduct their relationships when these are so diverse. What we are sure of, however, is that no trainer is an island. We all need a certain degree of emotional support as well as stimulation, challenge and formal sharing of information and decision-making responsibilities. Most 'classes' (lectures or skills groups) are conducted by single tutors, since it is not economically viable to employ two or more tutors to teach simultaneously. But some skill groups, community meetings and other forms of large groups are co-facilitated, and these arrangements allow trainers to observe each other in action and to offer feedback and support later. Trainers are much more often found collaborating in planning a syllabus, agreeing a timetable, discussing future plans or concerns about individual students. The BAC suggests that staff meetings are held regularly to review course procedures and developments. As well as having informal meetings with co-tutors (at home, over dinner or in the pub) you will of course hold more formal meetings with other staff from time to time, including necessary termly or annual meetings with your examining board, Head of department, marketing manager, external examiner, and others. While such formal occasions can come to feel like chores that you would rather avoid, do ensure that they are given due significance.

Co-tutors can be a source of warm support and nourishment. They can, however, be a source of difficulty. If you are a new or junior trainer, for example, and your more experienced and perhaps meticulous 'boss' begins to give you frequent negative advice, what will you do? If the fellow-trainer who seemed so well qualified and collaborative at the interview turns into a nervous, uncooperative colleague overnight, where do you stand? A great deal of successful training depends, in our experience, on flexibility, reliability, honesty and humour. You need to be able to count on colleagues. You need to be able to telephone them sometimes late at night in order to discuss a crisis or a nagging worry. Sometimes you may need a favour, for example someone willing to step in for you at short notice when you are sick. Tutors who are rigid in their commitments and unwilling to accommodate to any urgent needs are not always the best colleagues. Conversely, of course, colleagues who have no clear boundaries may telephone you all too often or become ill rather too much! Especially when you are working closely with a co-tutor, perhaps on a relatively small course, you need all the mutual understanding and cooperation you can get.

Again, this is an area in which there are clear ideals but frequent compromises. In your eagerness to work with a trainer who is readily available and apparently flexible, for example, you may assume that he or she has all the requisite knowledge and skills and understands his or her brief within the course. Before you know it, however, this trainer is teaching students not what you asked to be addressed but his or her own, favourite subjects which are somewhat at odds with the course orientation. Clear job descriptions can obviate such problems, but a certain amount of trust must generally be assumed. A more common scenario, but often quite difficult, occurs when co-tutors are compared by their students. Whether such comparisons are made informally, by gossip, or come as part of questionnaire feedback, it is sometimes the case that one tutor emerges as 'brilliant, stimulating, fascinating' and the other as 'dull, incompetent, disorganized'. This kind of reaction may be interpreted as a form of 'splitting' (all the bad feelings are projected on to one tutor, all the good on to the other) but it may simply reflect a great disparity in competency and popularity. What will you do? If this feedback is known to both of you, how will you react – emotionally, cognitively, interpersonally and professionally? We hope that most trainers would react in an enquiring and supportive manner; only when tutors receive consistently negative feedback is a serious investigation of their position warranted.

Key point

Reflect on the relationships between you and co-tutors, on how these relationships have been established, consider what you need from colleagues formally and informally and how you can best create and nurture good working relationships.

Epilogue

We hope that we have satisfactorily addressed and at least in some cases answered the questions posed by counsellor trainers. We would like to make the further observation, perhaps not so evident within the book, that the training task is also very rewarding. We have gained great pleasure from witnessing the real changes, both personal and professional, taking place in trainees over the course of time within training. It is a privilege to be involved in a learning environment of this kind, to get to know many trainees very well and to share with them in their aspirations to become skilful practitioners. There is also a good deal of affection and humour to be experienced as a counsellor trainer.

It is pleasing to see the growth of counselling and its availability to larger numbers of people. With the growth of counselling in private practice, in GPs' surgeries, in employee assistance programmes and community organizations, we hope to see an attendant debate on key questions on counsellor training. This debate would need to address the following: the current problems inherent in the existence of separate counselling and psychotherapy professions; the continuing proliferation of models of counselling and psychotherapy; the relative paucity of statutory, professional and academic agreement on training content and standards; the need for better research in the field; and the need to listen to the feedback from consumers and critics of counselling. It is perhaps natural for us to want to preserve our independence, diversity and creativity as trainers and counsellors, but this must be balanced by concern for greater effectiveness and commitment to ethical principles.

We draw readers' attention to the continuing work in Britain of the Standing Conference for the Advancement of Training and Supervision (SCATS). We also invite comments on the material presented here, and look forward to further collaboration with colleagues and students.

Appendices

1 BAC *Code of Ethics and Practice for Trainers*

Code of Ethics & Practice for Trainers of Counsellors

A. Code of Ethics
Introduction

The purpose of this Code of Ethics is to establish standards for trainers and to inform and protect members of the public seeking training as counsellors.

This document should be seen in relation to all other Codes of the Association.

Ethical standards of counsellors are derived from the values of integrity, impartiality and respect. Therefore trainers of counsellors work with their trainees in ways which enhance the trainees' ability to achieve appropriate standards of practice with regard to: respect for their clients' capacity for self-determination, confidentiality, competence and awareness of the boundaries of responsibility.

Trainers are experienced competent and practising counsellors who train people to become counsellors. Trainers endeavour to ensure that, when trainees complete the programme of training, the trainees have reached an appropriate level of competence. Trainees should be regularly assessed and informed of the results of these assessments.

The relationship between trainer and trainee is similar in some respects to that between counsellor and client, in that trainees, in the course of training, may find themselves in a vulnerable situation with regard to their trainer where painful and potentially damaging material may be revealed which needs to be handled in a sensitive and caring manner.

As adult learners, trainees bring their prior experience and personal style to the training. It is important that this is respected in ways which model good practice in counselling. Trainees are entitled to expect that they will only be challenged on matters which relate directly to the stated objectives of the training.

Trainers will be aware of the difference between training in counselling and training in counselling skills and should therefore direct students accordingly to appropriate courses.

A1. Issues of Responsibility

1.1 Training a person as a counsellor is a deliberately undertaken responsibility.

1.2 Trainers are responsible for the observance of the principles embodied in this Code of Ethics & Practice for Trainers and the other Codes of this Association.

1.3 Trainers must recognise the value and dignity of trainees irrespective of origin, status, gender, sexual orientation and age.

1.4 Trainers accept a responsibility to encourage and facilitate the self-development of trainees whilst also establishing clear boundaries and contracts to help trainees be responsible for their own continued learning, self-monitoring and development.

1.5 Trainers are responsible for setting, monitoring and modelling the boundaries between the training relationship and friendship or other relationships between themselves and the trainee.

1.6 Trainers are responsible for ensuring that they do not seek to satisfy their own emotional needs through relationships with their trainees.

1.7 Trainers must not engage in sexual activity with their trainees for the duration of the training programme, except where there is a pre-existing personal sexual relationship. In such cases it is not best practice to be on the same training programme. If this is unavoidable, and there is only one trainer, participants should be informed about the pre-existing personal relationship and care taken to monitor the group process.

1.8 The roles of trainee and client must be kept separate by the trainer. Should the need for counselling arise or be revealed during the course of training, trainers are responsible for suggesting and encouraging further in-depth personal work outside the course. This should be undertaken in a situation that is independent of the training assessment context.

A2. Issues of Competence

2.1 Trainers, should have considerable experience as counsellors, should commit themselves to undertake training as trainers, at regular intervals and/or seek ways of increasing their professional development and self-awareness.

2.2   Trainers should monitor and evaluate their training work and be able and willing to account to trainees and colleagues for what they do and why.

2.3   Trainers should regularly monitor and evaluate the limits of their competence as trainers by means of supervision or consultancy.

2.4   Trainers have a responsibility to themselves and to their trainees to monitor their own effectiveness, health and ability to train; to know when their personal resources are so depleted as to make it necessary for them to seek help and/or withdraw from counselling training whether temporarily or permanently.

B.   Code of Practice
Introduction

This Code of Practice provides more specific information and guidance regarding the implementation of the principles embodied in the Code of Ethics for Trainers.

B1.   Confidentiality

1.1   Trainers should inform trainees from the beginning of the course of all reasonably foreseeable circumstances in which confidentiality may be broken.

1.2   Confidentiality must be maintained with regard to information of a personal or sexual nature which is revealed during the training unless it is likely to contravene the BAC Codes of Ethics.

1.3   Information about specific trainees should not normally be used for publication in journals or meetings. If it is done then only with the trainee's permission and with anonymity being preserved when the trainee so specifies.

1.4   Discussion by trainers of their trainees with professional colleagues should be purposeful, relevant to the training, and not trivialising.

B2.   Management of the Work

2.1   Trainers should make basic information available to potential trainees before the start of the course, either in writing or by other appropriate means of communication. This should include:

a) the fees to be charged and any other expenses which may be incurred.

b) the dates and time commitments.

c) where selection procedures are in place the process by which decisions will be taken, including minimum entry requirements.

d) basic information about the content of the course, its philosophical and theoretical approach and the training methods to be used.

e) the qualifications of the trainers.

f) any requirements for supervision and work experience which the trainees will be expected to meet while on the course.

g) what assessment methods will be used during and at the end of the course.

h) the appeals procedure which trainees should follow if they are in dispute with trainers at the conclusion of the course.

2.2   It is desirable that there should be some consistency between the theoretical orientation of the course and the teaching methods used on it, eg. client-centred courses will tend to be trainee-centred.

2.3   Trainers have a responsibility to check with trainees before the course begins whether they are in therapy or counselling which may impede learning on the course.

2.4   Trainers need to suggest to their trainees that they consider their own needs for personal therapy or support outside the course and the contribution it might make to their work during their training programme.

2.5   Trainers should ensure that practical experience of counselling under regular supervision is part of counsellor training.

2.6   Trainers should arrange for initial, continuous, and final assessments of trainees' work and their continuing suitability for the course and possible need for personal therapy. Trainers should make trainees aware of this process, including the role of external assessors/examiners.

2.7   Trainers should ensure that trainees are given the opportunity to work on self awareness, individually, as well as in groups. Trainees need to learn to integrate professional practice and personal insights.

2.8   Trainers should ensure that trainees do not take on an ongoing counselling relationship with other members of the course. This does not exclude the need for peer group practice in pursuit of the course objectives.

2.9   Trainers should ensure that trainees are provided with the opportunity to give feedback about their experience of the training to the trainers at regular intervals during the course.

2.10 Trainers should encourage self assessment and peer assessment among their trainees.

2.11 Trainers should ensure that their trainees are made aware of the distinctions between counselling, managerial, and consultancy tasks and roles in training and supervision.

2.12 Trainers who become aware of a conflict between their obligation to a trainee and their obligation to the agency or organisation employing them should make explicit to the trainee the nature and existence of the conflict. The trainer should seek to resolve it if possible.

2.13 Where differences occur between a trainer and trainee which cannot be resolved, the trainer should consult with an independent consultant or external moderator.

2.14 Trainers should arrange for regular evaluation and assessment of their work by a supervisor or consultant experienced in training and should take account of their comments.

2   Sample assessment criteria

1 All students are expected to attend and participate in not less than 80 per cent of classes. In exceptional circumstances (for example, extended illness or other unforeseeable events), after discussion between tutors and those students not meeting the above attendance requirement, the opportunity may be offered to complete compensatory assignments or to repeat a year.

2 All students must complete written course assignments and meet the criteria for satisfactory levels of understanding and expression. 45 per cent will be considered a pass mark. Marks for written assignments will be averaged out at the end of each year. These will be considered alongside other course input (ongoing self-, peer- and tutor-assessment; tape-recordings) and a pass given where overall performance is judged to be satisfactory.

3 All students must submit a short tape-recorded example of their counselling, accompanied by a commentary, at the end of the

From: Thameslink Diploma in Counselling, Thameslink Healthcare Services NHS Trust, Dartford, Kent first year. In the event that this should prove unsatisfactory, the opportunity will be given for another tape-recording to be submitted following feedback on performance.

4 All students must submit a tape-recording of a full counselling session (45–50 minutes) accompanied by a transcript and explanatory commentary, by the end of the second year. 45 per cent will be the pass mark. Failure to satisfy tutors cannot be averaged out in this case, but a borderline submission may be resubmitted.

5 All students will be asked periodically throughout the course to give verbal and written self-reports on their own progress, including any areas in which they believe themselves to be in need of further work.

6 All students will be encouraged to give regular ongoing feedback to each other on competency in the use of counselling skills.

7 Tutors undertake to give ongoing verbal feedback to students on their competency in the use of counselling skills, indicating specific areas in which performance is in need of improvement.

8 In the event that any student is considered 'borderline' at the end of the first year, discussions between that student, a group of peers, and tutors, will be aimed at fair and constructive decisions as to ways forward or if necessary decisions to leave the course. In the event of dispute, the external examiner will be asked for guidance.

9 In the event that any student either at the end of the first or second year is considered not to have met satisfactory standards by tutors and by the external examiner, there will be no further right of appeal.

10 Any student who wishes to terminate at the end of the first year of the course, and whose work has met satisfactory standards, will be considered for the award of a discretionary Certificate in Counselling.

11 Students who are unable for any reason to complete the required minimum of 100 hours of formal counselling work with clients during the second year of the course, will be offered the opportunity, following discussion with tutors, of an extended period in which to complete this requirement, subject to satisfactory arrangements for supervision and accountability to course tutors.

12 Subject to overall satisfactory assessment, students will be awarded the Thameslink Diploma in Counselling at the end of (not less than) two years. In exceptional circumstances,

students achieving outstanding levels of competency in all assignments may be granted a 'distinction'.

3 Form for evaluation of seminar and tutor

Please fill out this questionnaire in the strictest confidence and anonymity. Please answer the questions as honestly and as precisely as possible. The information will be valuable in maintaining and improving the quality of education that you receive in this programme

Name of seminar _____
Name of tutor _____
Date/term of course _____

Please rate the following statements on a scale of 1–10 where 10 is the highest score and 1 is the lowest.

1 (a) . . . . Relevance of the seminar material to your own interests
  (b) . . . . Practical applicability
  (c) . . . . Structuring of seminar material
  (d) . . . . Seminar material put in historical, philosophical, and scientific context
  (e) . . . . Clarity of communication of seminar material
  (f) . . . . Time spent in class discussion
  (g) . . . . Encouragement of active class participation
  (h) . . . . Encouragement of critical debate
  (i) . . . . Challenge of your previous assumptions
  (j) . . . . Stimulus for reference to other sources
  (k) . . . . Assistance with academic research
  (l) . . . . Encouragement of your own style and creativity

2 Did you learn what you expected or hoped to learn? If not, why not?

From: M.A. in Psychotherapy and Counselling Regent's College, London

3 (a) ..... Tutor's awareness of class process
  (b) .... Tutor's sensitivity to wider issues
  (c) .... Tutors's objectivity; how prepared was the tutor to question his or her own point of view?
  (d) .... Tutor's awareness of new developments in the field
  (e) .... Tutor's openness to new developments in the field
  (f) .... Tutor's sensitivity to student's perspectives
  (g) .... Tutor's awareness of individual needs

4 Please describe any ways in which you think that this seminar could be improved.

5 Any other comments?

4   Evaluation of counsellor skills

Cognitive Therapy Scale

This scale is designed to provide a partial evaluation of a cognitive therapist. A separate instrument is being developed to assess, in much greater detail, the quality of the therapist's *conceptualization* and *strategy*; the evaluation will be based in part on a case summary and analysis submitted by the therapist. Furthermore, the scale is not intended to be used for the initial interview or final session with a patient.

Therapist: .... Patient:................ Date of session: ....
Tape ID number: ...... Rater:................. Date of rating:..............
Session number: .... ( ) Videotape   ( ) Audiotape   ( ) Live observation

Directions
For each item, assess the therapist on a scale from 0 to 6, and record the rating in the box next to the item heading. Descriptions are provided for even-numbered scale points. *If you believe the therapist falls between two of the descriptions, select the intervening odd number (1, 3, 5).* For example, if the therapist

From: Center for Cognitive Therapy, University of Pennsylvania set a very good agenda but did not establish priorities, assign a rating of 5 rather than 4 or 6.

If the descriptions for a given item occasionally do not seem to apply to the session you are rating, feel free to disregard them and use the more general scale below:

0	1	2	3	4	5	6
Poor	Barely adequate	Mediocre	Satisfactory	Good	Very good	Excellent

Please do not leave any item blank. For all items, focus on the skill of the therapist, taking into account how difficult the patient seems to be.

Part I General therapeutic skills

1 Agenda □

0 Therapist did not set agenda.
2 Therapist set agenda that was vague or incomplete.
4 Therapist worked with patient to set a mutually satisfactory agenda that included specific target problems (e.g. anxiety at work, dissatisfaction with marriage).
6 Therapist worked with patient to set an appropriate agenda with target problems, suitable for the available time. Established priorities and then followed the agenda.

2 Feedback □

0 Therapist did not ask for feedback to determine patient's understanding of, or response to, the session.
2 Therapist elicited some feedback from the patient, but did not ask enough questions to be sure the patient understood the therapist's line of reasoning during the session *or* to ascertain whether the patient was satisfied with the session.
4 Therapist asked enough questions to be sure that the patient understood the therapist's line of reasoning throughout the session and to determine the patient's reactions to the session. The therapist adjusted his/her behaviour in response to the feedback, when appropriate.
6 Therapist was especially adept at eliciting and responding to verbal and non-verbal feedback throughout the session (e.g. elicited reactions to session, regularly checked for understanding, helped summarize main points at end of session).

3 Understanding ☐

0 Therapist repeatedly failed to understand what the patient explicitly said and thus consistently missed the point. Poor empathic skills.
2 Therapist was usually able to reflect or rephrase what the patient explicitly said but repeatedly failed to respond to more subtle communication. Limited ability to listen and empathize.
4 Therapist generally seemed to grasp the patient's 'internal reality' as reflected by both what the patient explicitly said and what the patient communicated in more subtle ways. Good ability to listen and empathize.
6 Therapist seemed to understand the patient's 'internal reality' thoroughly and was adept at communicating this understanding through appropriate verbal and non-verbal responses to the patient (e.g. the tone of the therapist's response conveyed a sympathetic understanding of the patient's 'message'). Excellent listening and empathic skills.

4 Interpersonal effectiveness ☐

0 Therapist had poor interpersonal skills. Seemed hostile, demeaning, or in some other way destructive to the patient.
2 Therapist did not seem destructive, but had significant interpersonal problems. At times, therapist appeared unnecessarily impatient, aloof, insincere *or* had difficulty conveying confidence and competence.
4 Therapist displayed a *satisfactory* degree of warmth, concern, confidence, genuineness and professionalism. No significant interpersonal problems.
6 Therapist displayed *optimal* levels of warmth, concern, confidence, genuineness, and professionalism, appropriate for this particular patient in this session.

5 Collaboration ☐

0 Therapist did not attempt to set up a collaboration with patient.
2 Therapist attempted to collaborate with patient, but had difficulty *either* defining a problem that the patient considered important *or* establishing rapport.
4 Therapist was able to collaborate with patient, focus on a problem that both patient and therapist considered important, and establish rapport.
6 Collaboration seemed excellent; therapist encouraged patient as

much as possible to take an active role during the session (e.g. by offering choices) so they could function as a 'team.'

6 Pacing and efficient use of time ☐

0 Therapist made no attempt to structure therapy time. Session seemed aimless.
2 Session had some direction, but the therapist had significant problems with structuring or pacing (e.g. too little structure, inflexible about structure, too slowly paced, too rapidly paced).
4 Therapist was reasonably successful at using time efficiently. Therapist maintained appropriate control over flow of discussion and pacing.
6 Therapist used time very efficiently by tactfully limiting peripheral and unproductive discussion and by pacing the session as rapidly as was appropriate for the patient.

Part II Conceptualization, strategy, and technique

7 Guided discovery ☐

0 Therapist relied primarily on debate, persuasion, or 'lecturing'. Therapist seemed to be 'cross-examining' patient, putting the patient on the defensive, or forcing his/her point of view on the patient.
2 Therapist relied too heavily on persuasion and debate, rather than guided discovery. However, therapist's style was supportive enough that patient did not seem to feel attacked or defensive.
4 Therapist, for the most part, helped patient see new perspectives through guided discovery (e.g. examining evidence, considering alternatives, weighing advantages and disadvantages) rather than through debate. Used questioning appropriately.
6 Therapist was especially adept at using guided discovery during the session to explore problems and help patient draw his/her own conclusions. Achieved an excellent balance between skilful questioning and other modes of intervention.

8 Focusing on key cognitions or behaviours ☐

0 Therapist did not attempt to elicit specific thoughts, assumptions, images, meanings, or behaviours.
2 Therapist used appropriate techniques to elicit cognitions or behaviours; however, therapist had difficulty finding a focus *or* focused on cognitions/behaviours that were irrelevant to the patient's key problems.
4 Therapist focused on specific cognitions or behaviours relevant

to the target problems. However, therapist could have focused on more central cognitions or behaviours that offered greater promise for progress.

6 Therapist very skilfully focused on key thoughts, assumptions, behaviours, etc. that were most relevant to the problem area and offered considerable promise for progress.

9 Strategy for change ☐ [Note: For this time, focus on the quality of the therapist's strategy for change, not on how effectively the strategy was implemented or whether change actually occurred.]

0 Therapist did not select cognitive-behavioural techniques.

2 Therapist selected cognitive-behavioural techniques; however, either the overall strategy for bringing about change seemed vague *or* did not seem promising in helping the patient.

4 Therapist seemed to have a generally coherent strategy for change that showed reasonable promise and incorporated cognitive-behavioural techniques.

6 Therapist followed a consistent strategy for change that seemed very promising and incorporated the most appropriate cognitive-behavioural techniques.

10 Application of cognitive-behavioural techniques ☐ [Note: For this item, focus on how skilfully the techniques were applied, not on how appropriate they were for the target problem or whether change actually occurred.]

0 Therapist did not apply any cognitive-behavioural techniques.

2 Therapist used cognitive-behavioural techniques, but there were *significant flaws* in the way they were applied.

4 Therapist applied cognitive-behavioural techniques *with moderate skill.*

6 Therapist *very skilfully* and resourcefully employed cognitive-behavioural techniques.

11 Homework ☐

0 Therapist did not attempt to incorporate homework relevant to cognitive therapy.

2 Therapist had significant difficulties incorporating homework (e.g. did not review previous homework, did not explain homework in sufficient detail, assigned inappropriate homework).

4 Therapist reviewed previous homework and assigned 'standard' cognitive therapy homework generally relevant to issues dealt with in session. Homework was explained in sufficient detail.

6 Therapist reviewed previous homework and carefully assigned homework drawn from cognitive therapy for the coming week. Assignment seemed 'custom tailored' to help patient incorporate new perspectives, test hypotheses, experiment with new behaviours discussed during session, etc.

Part III Additional considerations

12 Problems ☐

(a) Did any special problems arise during the session (e.g. non-adherence to homework, interpersonal issues between therapist and patient, hopelessness about continuing therapy, relapse)?

Yes   No

(b) *If yes*:
0 Therapist could not deal adequately with special problems that arose.
2 Therapist dealt with special problems adequately, but used strategies or conceptualizations inconsistent with cognitive therapy.
4 Therapist attempted to deal with special problems using a cognitive framework and was *moderately skilful* in applying techniques.
6 Therapist was very skilful at handling special problems using cognitive therapy framework.

13 Unusual factors

Were there any significant unusual factors in this session that you feel justified the therapist's departure from the standard approach measured by this scale?

Yes (Please explain below)   No

Part IV Overall ratings and comments

14 Overall rating ☐

How would you rate the clinician overall in this session, as a cognitive therapist:

0	1	2	3	4	5	6
Poor	Barely Adequate	Mediocre	Satisfactory	Good	Very good	Excellent

15 Outcome study ☐

If you were conducting an outcome study in cognitive therapy, do you think you would select this therapist to participate at this time (assuming this session is typical)?

0	1	2	3	4
Definitely not	Probably not	Uncertain–borderline	Probably yes	Definitely yes

16 The patient ☐

How difficult did you feel this patient was to work with?

0	1	2	3	4	5	6
Not difficult, very receptive			Moderately difficult			Extremely difficult

17 Comments and suggestions for therapist's improvement

References

Abram, J. (1992) *Individual Psychotherapy Trainings*. London: Free Association Books.

Agazarian, Y. and Peters, R. (1981) *The Visible and Invisible Group*. London: Routledge and Kegan Paul.

ASC (1992) *Guide to Training Courses in Counselling* (3rd edn). Rugby: Association for Student Counselling/BAC.

Auerbach, A.A. and Johnson, N. (1977) 'Research on the therapist's level of experience', in A.S. Gurman and A.M. Razin (eds), *Effective Psychotherapy*. Oxford: Pergamon.

Aveline, M. (1990) 'Training and supervision of individual therapists', in W. Dryden (ed.), *Individual Therapy: A Handbook*. Milton Keynes: Open University Press.

Aveline, M. and Dryden, W. (eds) (1988) *Group Therapy in Britain*. Milton Keynes: Open University Press.

BAC (1990a) *The Recognition of Counsellor Training Courses*. Rugby: British Association for Counselling.

BAC (1990b) *Ramps Aren't Everything*. Rugby: British Association for Counselling.

Barrett-Lennard, G.T. (1962) 'Dimensions of therapist response as causal factors in therapeutic change', *Psychological Monographs*, 76, No. 43.

Bellack, A.S. and Hersen, M. (eds) (1990) *Handbook of Comparative Treatments for Adult Disorders*. New York: Wiley.

Beutler, L.E. (1979) 'Toward specific psychological therapies for specific conditions', *Journal of Consulting and Clinical Psychology*, 47 (5): 882–97.

Beutler, L.E., Crago, M. and Arizmendi, T.G. (1986) 'Therapist variables in psychotherapy process and outcome', in S.L. Garfield and A.E. Bergin (eds), *Handbook of Psychotherapy and Behavior Change* (3rd edn). New York: Wiley.

Bond, T. (1991) *HIV Counselling*. Rugby: BAC.

Bond, T. (1993) *Standards and Ethics for Counselling in Action*. London: Sage.

Borger, R. and Seabourne, A.E.M. (1966) *The Psychology of Learning*. Harmondsworth: Penguin.

BPS (1993) *Regulations for the Diploma in Counselling Psychology*. Leicester: British Psychological Society.

Clarkson, P. and Gilbert, M. (1991) 'The training of counsellor trainers and supervisors', in W. Dryden and B. Thorne (eds), *Training and Supervision for Counselling in Action*. London: Sage.

Dainow, S. and Bailey, C. (1988) *Developing Skills with People*. Chichester: Wiley.

Dryden, W. (ed.) (1990) *Individual Therapy: A Handbook*. Milton Keynes: Open University Press.

Dryden, W. (1991a) *Towards Integration: A Dialogue with John Norcross*. Buckingham: Open University Press.

Dryden, W. (1991b) *Dryden on Counselling. Vol. 3: Training and Supervision*. London: Whurr.

Dryden, W. (1992) *The Dryden Interviews: Dialogues on the Psychotherapeutic Process*. London: Whurr.

Dryden, W. (1993) *Reflections on Counselling*. London: Whurr.

Dryden, W. and Feltham, C. (1992) *Brief Counselling: A Practical Guide for Beginning Practitioners*. Buckingham: Open University Press.

Dryden, W. and Hill, L.K. (eds) (1993) *Innovations in Rational-Emotive Therapy*. London: Sage.

Dryden, W. and Spurling, L. (eds) (1989) *On Becoming a Psychotherapist*. London: Routledge.

Dryden, W. and Thorne, B. (eds) (1991) *Training and Supervision for Counselling in Action*. London: Sage.

Egan, G. (1990) *Exercises in Helping Skills: A Training Manual to Accompany 'The Skilled Helper'*. Pacific Grove, CA: Brooks/Cole.

Falloon, V. (1992) *How to Get More Clients*. London: Brainwave.

Feltham, C. (1993) 'What are the difficulties in making a living as a counsellor?', in W. Dryden (ed.), *Questions and Answers on Counselling in Action*. London: Sage.

Ford, J.D. (1979) 'Research on training counselors and clinicians', *Review of Educational Research*, 49: 87–130.

Frances, A., Sweeney, J. and Clarkin, J. (1985) 'Do psychotherapies have specific effects?', *American Journal of Psychotherapy*, 39 (2): 159–74.

Garfield, S.L. and Bergin, A.E. (eds) (1986) *Handbook of Psychotherapy and Behavior Change* (3rd edn). New York: Wiley.

Guy, J.D. (1987) *The Personal Life of the Psychotherapist*. New York: Wiley.

Hargie, O.D.W. and Gallagher, M.S. (1992) 'A comparison of the core conditions of client-centred counselling in real and role-play counselling episodes', *Counselling*, 3 (3): 153–7.

Hart, L.B. (1991) *Training Methods That Work*. London: Kogan Page.

Haynes, M.E. (1988) *Effective Meeting Skills*. London: Kogan Page.

Heather, N. and Robertson, I. (1989) *Problem Drinking*. Oxford: Oxford University Press.

Heron, J. (1989) *The Facilitator's Handbook*. London: Kogan Page.

Heron, J. (1991) *Helping the Client*. London: Sage.

Hill, C.E. (1989) *Therapist Techniques and Client Outcomes*. Newbury Park, CA: Sage.

Honey, P. and Mumford, A. (1982) *The Manual of Learning Styles*. Maidenhead: Honey.

Hugman, R. (1987) 'Monitoring community social work placements', *Issues in Social Work Education*, 7 (2): 115–28.

Inskipp, F. (1986) *Counselling: The Trainer's Handbook*. Cambridge: National Extension College.

Ivey, A.E. (1987) *Intentional Interviewing and Counseling*. Monterey, CA: Brooks/Cole.

Ivey, A.E., Ivey, M.B. and Simek-Downing, L. (1980) *Counseling and Psychotherapy: Integrating Skills, Theory and Practice*. Englewood Cliffs, NJ: Prentice-Hall.

Jacobs, M. (1991) *Insight and Experience: A Manual of Training in the Technique and Theory of Psychodynamic Counselling and Therapy*. Milton Keynes: Open University Press.

Maeder, T. (1990) *Children of Psychiatrists and Other Psychotherapists*. New York: Harper and Row.

Masson, J. (1991) *Against Therapy.* New York: Atheneum.

Mearns, D. and Thorne, B. (1988) *Person-centred Counselling in Action.* London: Sage.

Millar, R., Crute, V. and Hargie, O. (1992) *Professional Interviewing.* London: Routledge.

Newman, F. (1991) *The Myth of Psychology.* New York: Castillo.

Noonan, E. and Spurling, L. (eds) (1992) *The Making of a Counsellor.* London: Routledge.

Osborne, J. (1987) 'A human science study of learning about "learning"', *Journal of Humanistic Psychology,* 27 (4): 485–500.

OUP (1979) *Preparing to Study.* Milton Keynes: Open University Press.

Pilgrim, D. (1992) 'Psychotherapy and political evasions', in W. Dryden and C. Feltham (eds), *Psychotherapy and its Discontents.* Buckingham: Open University Press.

Pitts, J.H. (1992) 'Counselor preparation: organizing a practicum and internship program in counselor education', *Counselor Education and Supervision,* 31 (4): 196–207.

Proctor, B. (1991) 'On being a trainer', in W. Dryden and B. Thorne (eds), *Training and Supervision for Counselling in Action.* London: Sage.

Progoff, I. (1975) *At a Journal Workshop.* New York: Dialogue House.

Purton, C. (1991) 'Selection and assessment in counsellor training courses', in W. Dryden and B. Thorne (eds), *Training and Supervision for Counselling in Action.* London: Sage.

Rae, L. (1986) *The Skills of Training.* Aldershot: Wildwood House.

Reid, M.A., Barrington, H. and Kenney, J. (1992) *Training Interventions: Managing Employee Development* (3rd edn). London: Institute of Personnel Management.

Robertiello, R.C. and Schoenewolf, G. (1987) *101 Common Therapeutic Blunders.* New York: Aronson.

Russell, R.K., Crimmings, A.M. and Lent, R.W. (1984) 'Counselor training and supervision: theory and research', in S.D. Brown and R.W. Lent (eds), *Handbook of Counseling Psychology.* New York: Wiley.

Russell, J., Dexter, G. and Bond, T. (1992) *Differentiation Between Advice, Guidance, Befriending, Counselling Skills and Counselling.* Discussion paper 1. Welwyn, Herts: Advice, Guidance and Counselling Lead Body.

Smithies, D. (1987) *How to Speak in Public.* London: Unwin.

Thomas, B. (1992) *Total Quality Training.* London: McGraw-Hill.

Thorne, B. (1989) 'The blessing and the curse of empathy', in W. Dryden and L. Spurling (eds), *On Becoming a Psychotherapist.* London: Routledge.

Truax, C.B. and Carkhuff, R.R. (1967) *Toward Effective Counseling and Psychotherapy.* Chicago: Aldine.

Varah, C. (ed.) (1985) *The Samaritans: Befriending the Suicidal.* London: Constable.

Williams, R. (1992) 'A trainer's first steps', *Counselling,* 3 (1): 20–2.

Woodhouse, D. and Pengelly, P. (1991) *Anxiety and the Dynamics of Collaboration.* Aberdeen: Aberdeen University Press.

Index